MAN VS MIND

Daniel C. Richardson is a Reader in Experimental Psychology at University College London. Prior to that, he was an undergraduate at Magdalen College, Oxford; a graduate student at Cornell; a postdoctoral researcher at Stanford; and an assistant professor at the University of California, Santa Cruz. His research examines how individuals' thought processes are related to the people around them. He has authored many scientific articles in cognitive, developmental and social psychology, and has appeared on both 'Duck Quacks Don't Echo' and Al Jazeera. He received two Provost's Teaching Awards from UCL, and has performed shows combining science, music and live experiments in museums, pubs and theatres.

MAN VS MIND

EVERYDAY PSYCHOLOGY EXPLAINED

Daniel C. Richardson

Illustrated by Joe Lyward

Aurum
Press

Brimming with creative inspiration, how-to projects and useful information to enrich your everyday life, Quarto Knows is a favourite destination for those pursuing their interests and passions. Visit our site and dig deeper with our books into your area of interest: Quarto Creates, Quarto Cooks, Quarto Homes, Quarto Lives, Quarto Drives, Quarto Explores, Quarto Gifts, or Quarto Kids.

First published in 2017 by Aurum Press
an imprint of The Quarto Group
The Old Brewery, 6 Blundell Street
London N7 9BH
United Kingdom

www.QuartoKnows.com

A catalogue record for this book is available from the British Library.

ISBN 978 1 78131 670 2
Ebook ISBN 978 1 78131 764 8

10 9 8 7 6 5 4 3 2 1
2021 2020 2019 2018 2017

Illustrations and design by Joe Lyward

Printed by CPI Group (UK) ltd, Croydon, CR0 4YY

FSC
www.fsc.org
MIX
Paper from
responsible sources
FSC® C020471

Contents

Introduction

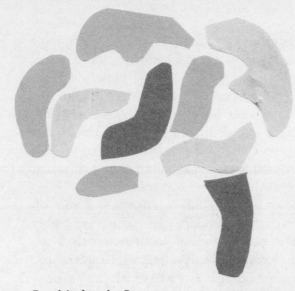

In this book, I want to uncover some of the strange and surprising features of human thought and the ways we behave. This isn't a textbook where we traipse through each field of psychology in turn, like a diligent tourist visiting every site in the guidebook. Instead, each chapter begins with a simple question, then we'll look across all areas of psychology to find a scientific answer.

These questions may seem quite random, but through them you'll learn about cutting-edge research in neuroscience and psychology, as well as the classic insights into our minds that psychologists have known for decades, but are still mostly unheard of outside our field. I also hope you'll gain an appreciation of how we use the tools of science to understand the human mind, what we can conclude from our evidence and, just as importantly, what we cannot.

Let's start with the first question: why does the kakapo exist? Bright green and too fat to fly, it's a parrot that waddles around the forests of New Zealand. When kakapos decide to start a family, the male emits a loud bass rumble to attract a female. Unfortunately, it takes a lot of energy to produce this noise – think how large the bass speakers are in a club – so the male kakapo can only sing his love song once every two-to-four years, when a particular tree drops a particular nutrient-rich fruit on the ground, the only place the bird can reach. The problem for the female kakapo is that it's really hard to know where the bass sound is coming from.

If they do manage to find each other, a pair of kakapos may eventually produce eggs, which are highly sought after as a meal by various small mammals. They are drawn by the kakapos' musty odour, which apparently resembles an old violin case. If a weasel attacks the nest, the kakapo has a defence: it stands very still with its wings spread out in an attempt to cover the eggs, but allowing the weasel to help itself.

The kakapo is one of the most charmingly inept creatures on this planet. They are so poor at the art of survival that only a handful exist; each kakapo actually has a team of people dedicated to keeping it alive. Here's the puzzle: the kakapo evolved to be this way. These flightless birds are winners in the survival of the fittest. So why on earth would evolution produce such a hot mess of a creature?

The key to understanding the kakapo is where it lives. Or rather, when. It evolved in New Zealand, a place that was covered in fruit-bearing trees for thousands of years. The kakapos didn't have to wait for a couple of years between feeds, and they were plentiful enough that females didn't have to trek through the forest to find a bass call because potential mates were thick on the ground. For thousands of years, kakapos did not have any predatory land mammals that would eat their eggs (those would arrive with human settlers). The only predator that threatened the birds' happy existence was a large eagle. Therefore, if you live in a forest and have green feathers, a good defence against an overhead predator is to stand very still and cover your nest with your wings.

The kakapo is a highly specialised animal, perfectly evolved for a world that no longer exists. In many ways, we too are like the kakapo. Human beings evolved in a world with a particular habitat, in social groups of a particular size, with behaviours and diets perfectly suited to the challenges and opportunities around us. We no longer live in that world. Now we live in habitats of high-population densities, with nutrition tailored to our desires, rather than our needs, and engage in activities such as reading, writing and operating machinery that were alien to our species until fairly recently in human history.

We live in an illusion of rationality. It is possible for us to make reasoned, sensible choices, illuminated by carefully collected evidence, so we feel that most of our decisions are rational and enlightened. However, we did not evolve to be rational and sensible. Like the kakapo, we evolved in response to different pressures. Our brains were shaped for a different purpose.

In this book, we'll see that some of our fundamental beliefs about thought simply aren't borne out by psychological science. People do not always like things – jobs, partners, or products – that are rewarding. We do not like choice. Our eyes do not deliver an accurate view of the world and our memory is not there to record it. Although we believe in fairness, equality and tolerance, our minds are built for prejudice, assumption and bias. This doesn't mean we are stupid or poorly evolved. It means that, just like the hapless kakapo, we are built for a different world.

Our social networks now expand across the globe. Our micro-behaviour and biology is constantly monitored by smart technology we install in our homes and wear on our bodies, and we can have our individual genome read as easily as tea leaves. To understand the impact of this new technology, we have to understand the lumbering humans that are plugged into it. That's what we'll explore in this book. How do we form social connections to other people? What does our behaviour tell us about our thoughts? How do our genes determine who we are? Each chapter will begin with a simple question, and end by giving insight into your own mind, the people around you and how we all will fit into the new world emerging around us.

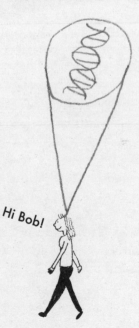

Mind vs mind

Where are our thoughts?

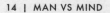

Our imagination, dreams, hopes, fears and loves, our understanding of distant galaxies, our knowledge of every contestant in *Celebrity Big Brother*. Are all these things really just the activity of a cluster of cells about the size of a disappointingly small pumpkin? How can thoughts be generated by something physical? Where exactly do they reside?

Try the following exercise, or ask the nearest person to you. (This is particularly good to do on an aeroplane. You'll either have an interesting conversation or you'll guarantee that they won't speak to you again for the duration of the flight: either way, a win.) Point to where your thinking happens. If you are like most people, you'll gesture vaguely towards your head. However, what evidence do you have for that belief? I'm asking for direct, personal experience. Unless you are a neuroscientist, you can't say anything about brain-imaging experiments. What makes us think that thoughts reside in the head?

People's answers tend to distil into a few categories. Maybe it's just a cultural or linguistic habit. We speak about 'keeping things under your hat', 'keeping your head', and so on. Therefore, it's just a belief that we pass on. Or perhaps it's from the senses – our eyes and ears surround the head, so it seems as if that is the perceptual focal point of our experiences. It could be from biological design. Dense bone surrounds and protects your brain, suggesting that it's pretty important to keep safe.

Throughout this first chapter, we will be sidling up to one idea in particular: what the neuroscientist Francis Crick called, in his book of the same title, 'the astonishing hypothesis'. A version of this sentiment has been bandied about since the ancient Greeks, and the seventeenth-century philosopher Baruch Spinoza was a big fan. It's worth reading in Crick's prose:

> 'You, your joys and your sorrows, your memories and your ambitions, your sense of personal identity and free will, are in fact no more than the behaviour of a vast assembly of nerve cells and their associated molecules.'

We will discuss the evidence and implications of Crick's astonishing hypothesis, tracing the struggle of man versus mind through the ages. We'll look back through history for different answers to the question of where thought lies, from ancient Egyptians to modern neuroscientists. In addition, we'll look at the reasons people had for locating the mind in particular parts of the body, and how we can reconcile ideas about the soul and conscious thought with emerging knowledge of the brain and nervous system.

From heart to head

In ancient Egypt, the heart was the centre of the self. They reasoned that it was right in the centre of the body, connected to everything by the veins. The heart develops first in the foetus. If you get an injury to the heart, even the tiniest nick from an arrow, you die. In contrast, you can get a blow to the head, and even have large chunks of your brain destroyed, yet still be a living, mostly functional person. The Egyptians thought the brain was unimportant – they called it 'head marrow' and guessed that it might be used to cool the blood. When a corpse was embalmed, they would yank out the brains using a bit of long bit of wire inserted up the nose and toss them aside as a treat for the cats.

While ancient Greeks such as the philosopher-scientist Aristotle concurred with the Egyptian view, a second-century philosopher-physician called Galen traced the nerves (rather than the blood vessels) and found that they all ended up at the brain. He argued that they were related to controlling the body, and demonstrated the point by severing the nerves of a lion, removing its ability to roar.

During the Renaissance, the drawings of the anatomist Andreas Vesalius and the polymath Leonardo

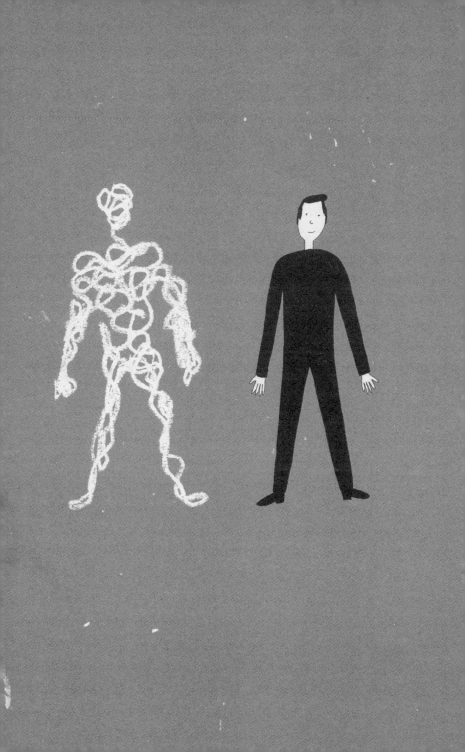

da Vinci provided new insights into the structure of the brain, with intricate drawings of its ventricles, the gaps and holes that ran through it. The philosopher René Descartes imagined that these ventricles were like the pipes of a church organ; the soul was a type of wind flowing through and thoughts were the music it played.

However, in Descartes' view the mind and the brain were fundamentally different things. He argued that there are objects in the world that are material, physical and spatial (that which scientists can measure and weigh) and there are things that are non-physical and non-material (the mind, thoughts and the soul). Descartes thought that, for each of us, our non-material soul interacts with our physical body via a tiny structure at the centre of the brain called the pineal gland. His basic notion of dualism – that mental things are different to physical things – remains influential today. It is endorsed by most religious viewpoints that have some notion of the soul or afterlife, or believe that human beings are more than their earthly bodies. It is also in direct conflict with Crick's astonishing hypothesis: that we are simply the activity of cells.

Since Descartes, scientists have tried to locate mental function within the matter of the brain, rather than the realm of the soul. Anatomists in the 1600s, such as Thomas Willis and Nicolaus Steno, agreed that signals – the decision to move one's hand, for example – were passing through the nerves. So what form did these signals take? Descartes had imagined the soul gusting through the ventricles of the brain, but the nerves throughout the body were not hollow. Perhaps nerves were like violin strings, transmitting information as vibration? They seemed too soft and pulpy, though.

Perhaps thoughts were transmitted by a fluid? If so, scientists reasoned that if you put your hand in a beaker of water and decided to open and close your fist, the water level in the beaker should rise as you sent those fluid signals to your hand. To test it, they constructed tables carefully balanced like a seesaw. The scientists lay on the tables and thought really hard, expecting the table to tilt head-down, as the nerve-fluid rushed to the brain. These experiments, logical and ingenious as they were, failed to find the means by which nerves transmitted thought throughout the body. They were looking in the wrong place.

It's alive!

History has lost the exact circumstances under which we discovered the true means of a thought becoming an action, but it is said to involve some combination of a table, a blunt knife and a dead frog. In 1780, the physician Luigi Galvani was in the kitchen while some frogs were being prepared for dinner. The blunt knife needed to be sharpened and cleaned, and doing so on this occasion imparted a static electric charge to the blade. Galvani noticed that when the blade touched the leg of the frog, the dead animal twitched, as if its puppeteer had suddenly woken.

Many frogs later, Galvani had demonstrated in careful experiments that the nerves of frogs and other animals communicated by electrical discharge. He and other scientists graduated from rubbing static charges in metal to rigging up lightning conductors during storms to show the power of electricity over flesh.

It's hard now to appreciate the significance of this moment. The dominant view then, as now, was that the mind was something mystical, a world apart from physical matter. Yet here, scientists had shown that the mysteries of willpower and the mind's control of the body were somehow reducible to electrical phenomena and could be measured and controlled. In the following years, Galvani's nephew, Giovanni Aldini, even reanimated the corpse of an executed criminal in London. It was early experiments such as these that the writer Mary Shelley had read about before she wrote her gothic horror novel *Frankenstein*, capturing the fear and philosophical shock of these discoveries.

Electricity was the essence of life, or its means of transmission, at least. It was the difference between a living and a dead body. But how does the brain generate and process these electrical impulses? At the end of the nineteenth century, scientists developed the means to stain brain cells so they could be viewed individually under a microscope. They discovered the neuron, and realised that the brain is made up of a dense network of these cells relaying electrical signals to each other.

Now we know there are approximately 80–100 billion neurons of various shapes and sizes in the brain. Each cell body has a long cable that sends out a signal, known as an axon, and a set of feathery, branching extensions called dendrites that receive signals from other axons. Where each axon and dendrite meets, there is a gap called a synapse, and each neuron has around 7,000 synapses. Chemicals called neurotransmitters flow across the synapse to transmit the electrical signals. The strength of the connection across the synapse can alter each time it is used, so that each time the axon fires a signal, the synapse has a slightly different response. This is learning. Brain activity is 80 billion interconnected processing units, each relaying electrical activity to 7,000 of its neighbours, all changing their responses with each wave of activity, learning and adapting to input.

Walking cats and dreaming rats

We can measure the brain's electrical activity with the same device that an electrician would use to test a circuit. Small probes can be inserted into brain tissue and the electrical signal of cells can be measured. In the 1950s neurophysiologists David Hubel and Torsten Wiesel did this first with cats who were awake. They passed a black line on a white card in front of a cat's eyes and measured activity from a particular cell that fired only if the line was horizontal and in a particular location.

More recently, neuroscientist John O'Keefe and his colleagues inserted clusters of probes, each finer than a human hair, into a brain structure known as the hippocampus – in this instance, using rats. The animals wore the device while running through a maze. After they felt at home in the maze, the researchers noticed that when a rat was in a particular location, the same cell in the hippocampus would fire; at another location, a different cell. They realised that these clusters of hippocampal cells had encoded spatial locations. The researchers were using an electrical probe to directly record a rat's mental image of its environment.

Later researchers continued to investigate these 'place cells', as they became known. As technology advanced, the sensors were small enough to be left in the rat. One lab at the Massachusetts Institute of Technology continued to record from them while a rat was sleeping. At one point while the rat slept, the hippocampal cells sparked into life. The cells coding for particular places in the maze were active in the correct order, as if the rat were wandering from corridor to corridor in its mind. The researchers made a tentative hypothesis: they were recording the rat's dreams.

Scientists can now do more than just snoop around a rat's subconscious – they can direct it. In one experiment, a rat runs around a maze that is set up with a junction at one location. If it runs left, it hears a bong sound; if it turns right, a ping sound. It explores the maze, building up its mental map of it, as the sensors record from its place cells. While it sleeps, the researchers eavesdrop on the rat's dreams once more. They wait until the place cell that coded for the location of the junction fires – when the rat, in its dream, is about to choose left or right. They play a bong, which the sleeping rat can hear, and in its dream the rat obediently turns left. The researchers can tell that is where the rat is in its dream because all the place cells for walking down the left corridor fire in turn. Science can both record and control the dreams of rats.

Talking heads

For the past hundred years, neuroscience has been asking not only how the brain transmits information and impulses, but where in the brain particular mental functions are located. For example, in rats and humans, we now know that the hippocampus is heavily involved in spatial representations and memory.

From the middle of the nineteenth century onwards, physicians began to notice systematic patterns between patients' mental symptoms and damage to particular locations in their brains, revealed later in autopsies. This trauma could be caused by violent injury (back then, there were a lot of wars producing useful data), by tumours, or by strokes – tiny explosions in the vessels supplying blood to the brain. In some hospitals, when a new patient couldn't speak, had lost their memory, or only shaved on one side of their face, physicians would even place bets on where in the brain the autopsy would discover damaged tissue.

Carefully compiled, systematic patient data led to the development of maps of the brain, with each lobe and wrinkle tied to mental functions: vision in the occipital lobe at the back of the head, language in the temporal lobe above the ears, and so on. However, the maps were more fine-grained than that. Damage in one area of the brain would take out a patient's ability to speak fluently, with every word painfully drawn out (a bit like how I used to attempt to speak French at school). Injury to a different area would leave speech production intact, but the patient might produce a fluent stream of near-gibberish (a bit like how I now speak French after a few glasses of wine). As each patient was studied, tiny regions of the brain were tied to specific mental functions.

One problem with this endeavour was that it led to the development of phrenology. Some Victorian scientists argued that if particular mental functions were related to specific regions of the brain, then it was logical that the shape of one's head was indicative of a personality or mental ability. None of this is at all true, but the concept became a sideshow spectacle, with practitioners 'reading' people's heads to diagnose their personalities. It culminated in the familiar white china heads that are still on sale today as novelty gifts, with regions of the scalp marked as 'spirituality', 'cautiousness', and so on.

This is all nonsense of course, and irritates psychologists in the way that astrology irritates astronomers. The other side of phrenology was very much less amusing, as it fed into the theories of eugenics put forward by people such as Francis Galton. They argued, for example, that differences in the shape of heads that could be observed between black Africans and white Europeans, were indicative of a moral and rational superiority that justified the slave trade. This is simply racism ladled on top of bad science, but such ideas shaped the immigration policies of the United States and fuelled the ideologies of British imperialists and, later on, the Nazis.

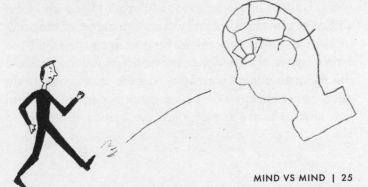

There is no evidence that the shape of one's head is indicative of anything other than hat size. Phrenology was a dead end. However, many of the names and functions of brain regions first identified by the early anatomists are still in use today. Often, though, our understanding of their functions has been revised. The reason for this is that patient symptoms are not the most reliable indication of impairment location. Firstly, brain injuries can be messy things and rarely damage just one region alone. Secondly, when treating a patient, earlier physicians were not just observing a symptom, but observing a person who had learnt how to cope with a symptom, which is not the same thing. We now know that the brain has a surprising degree of plasticity: cells in the brain can take on different functions in response to damage or changing input. All this complicates the relationship between a brain injury and a patient's observable behaviour.

Mapping the brain

Our understanding of brain localisation has benefitted most from the remarkable technologies we now use to study psychological function in awake and healthy individuals. The same sort of probe used by John O'Keefe can also be used to send a charge, stimulating cells in a similar manner to how Galvani twitched the frog's leg. In the 1940s, neurosurgeon Wilder Penfield did this with human patients who were undergoing brain surgery for epilepsy. Once the skull was open, Penfield was able to probe the exposed surface of the brain in a conscious patient. There are no pain sensors in the brain, so it didn't hurt them. He found that stimulating different locations could make specific muscles twitch, and even evoke certain memories in his patients. One woman reported that she thought she heard a mother calling out to her small children when a particular cell was jiggled with electrical current.

There are now many ways to peer inside the skull to see the brain at work, from injecting a patient with radioactive matter and tracking its dispersal, to shining a near-infrared light through the skull to see how the blood flow scatters the light. The most commonly used technique is a form of magnetic resonance imaging (MRI).

During an MRI scan, the patient lies on a table and is fed into what looks like a huge white doughnut. This houses a massive electromagnet capable of generating a magnetic field perhaps 50,000 times greater than that of the Earth. Just like the comic book character Magneto, this machine can pull metal objects across the room, so it's very important to remove any piercings you might have before going into an MRI scanner, before they are literally torn out of you.

The magnetic field lines up the nuclei of hydrogen atoms inside the patient's body, which are usually scattered randomly. Together, these lined-up atoms produce a magnetic signal themselves that can be measured by the MRI sensors. A slightly different signal can be coaxed out of atoms in different types of tissue, so an MRI can scan from lots of directions and positions and build up a 3D image of the body's internal structure.

A functional MRI (fMRI) can go one better and reveal not just the internal anatomy, but also how it is working. The signal from the hydrogen atoms in oxygenated blood is different to the signal from deoxygenated blood, so an fMRI machine can track that difference to measure how blood flow is changing across the brain while the mind is put to work.

As a result of this remarkable technology, a patient can sit in a fMRI machine and perform a mental task while the scanner maps the blood flow in their brain, and hence, the activity of neurons. One such task could be listening to sounds. What researchers typically find is that during this listening task, almost all brain cells are active in one way or another, in which case they can give a second task. Now, the patient might listen to sounds that are words in their native language, and the brain activity is mapped again. The researchers look at the difference between the two maps of brain activation for the two tasks, subtracting one from the other. They then reason that what they are left with are the areas of the brain that are specific to processing language. These are not the brain areas dealing broadly with listening, processing sound, feeling a bit bored, lying still, worrying about having removed piercings, and all the other things that might be going through someone's head – all these things can be assumed to have happened in both tasks. By subtracting the activation maps from each other, they can look at those brain areas specialised for language processing alone.

The 'ten per cent' myth

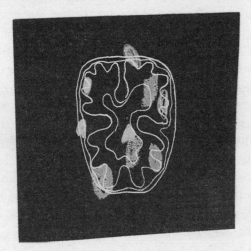

If you have seen pictures of brains with glowing dots showing active brain areas, this is probably how they were produced. You can run experiments showing people pictures of familiar faces, and then pictures of faces of people they love, and argue that the differences between them are the brain regions that specialise in love. Accordingly, you might see a newspaper article saying something along the lines of, 'scientists claim that this is the brain region associated with envy/addiction/ belief in God', accompanied by a picture of a brain with glowing dots in certain places. Remember, though, that fMRI studies subtract activation maps from each other. Whenever you feel envy, addiction or God, your whole brain is active – not just those little dots produced by subtracting one scan from another.

This common misunderstanding of pictures of brain activation might be one reason for the most prominent, incredibly wrong, embarrassingly misguided 'fact' about neuroscience: we only use ten per cent of our brains. This is not just a little bit wrong. Nor is it true in only some ways. It's completely wrong and against everything we know about the brain. If you said to a neuroscientist that science says we only use ten per cent of our brains, it would be akin to telling an astronomer that science reckons the sun is moved around the sky by a great big space goat. Your brain draws an incredible twenty per cent of your body's energy as it is. If that was how much it used at ten per cent, then running it at even fifty per cent would require shutting down all of your other organs.

Maybe one reason people believe this is that the physicist Albert Einstein once said that people only ever achieve ten per cent of their potential. Sadly, that could be true. Einstein certainly wasn't making a statement about the brain, though. Another reason is perhaps that fMRI pictures with little glowing dots showing brain functions specialised to particular tasks give the impression that most of the time ninety per cent of the brain is grey and inert. It isn't. It is buzzing away and active all the time during the aforementioned language processing task, for example. It was also active during the non-language task, so didn't get coloured. In fact, if ninety per cent of your brain was inactive most of the time, then those cells would quickly wither and die and your head would smell of week-old sushi.

The fMRI is an astonishing technique that allows us to map mental function onto brain activity in a way that would have blown Descartes' mind. However, its limitations are important to understand. For one thing, such experiments are limited to things that fMRI can show, as well as things a patient can do while lying down as still as possible on a bench inside an electromagnet. For another, fMRI machines distinguish one-second periods of activity within tiny, millimetre-cubed regions – very coarse measures on the scale of the brain. Within each of those minute regions of space there could be half a million neurons, with all sorts of activity over that one second.

This scale problem makes it hard to appreciate both how far we've come with understanding the brain and how much further we have to go. We can recognise that getting to the moon was a big deal, and how much harder it will be to reach the stars. For the brain – a lump of tissue the size of your cupped hands – now that we can measure neuron activity, there is little barrier to equating mind and brain. However, there are just so many densely interconnected neurons that science is nowhere near answering some pretty basic questions about it. An fMRI machine can't read our thoughts; it can't tell us if someone is lying. We can scan someone's body and guess at their heart and muscle function, but we can't fMRI a brain and tell if someone is smart or creative.

Mind vs man

So how close are we to accepting Crick's 'astonishing hypothesis' that all our thoughts are 'no more than the behaviour of a vast assembly of nerve cells and their associated molecules'? We have figured out how signals are sent through the nerves to the body, and that billions of tiny cells communicate in the same way. At a basic level, we can look at the activity of millions of them at a time and relate it to types of mental processing. In rats, at least, we can eavesdrop on dreams and manipulate them. Perhaps with technological advances we will soon have the same resolution and control over human neurons. That said, I think that many will still not accept Crick's astonishing hypothesis. The barrier is not the scientific problem of understanding the vast assembly of nerve cells, hard as that is. It is the human problem of admitting that this is all we are.

Are all our thoughts 'no more than the behaviour of a vast assembly of nerve cells and their associated molecules'?

Mind vs sight

Is the eye a camera?

There are obscure or complex functions to many parts of the human body that science is only just figuring out, such as the appendix, the cortex of the brain and men's nipples. However, the eyeball seems a lot more straightforward. It's a camera: you point it at things and it converts light into an image. These images are then stored in the mind, much like a camera does on a reel of film or a memory card. We share the words we have for perception with photography – lenses, focusing, memory storage, and so on. Understanding of human perception rests on the metaphor that the eye is like a camera, and that something that has been seen can be recalled, as if looking back through a photo album. Let's take that metaphor at face value and pick it apart. Does it stand up to the latest evidence from biology, human behaviour and psychology?

The answer suggests that we need to reconfigure our understanding of what the eye is designed to do. The implications of this extend far beyond the eyeball to a re-evaluation of the function of perception itself, and the hazy, indefinite relationship between the real world around us and what we actually experience of it. The gap between visual input from your eyes and your perceptual experience of the world is bridged by the bluff and guesswork of your brain.

Any review of a new phone will probably include a discussion about the quality of its camera – the number of megapixels, its sensitivity to light and motion, and the power of the lens. It might also include some example pictures and ask if they match what the camera was pointing at. Are there any artefacts or errors introduced by the camera? Do skin tones appear correctly? Are details lost in the shadows?

Here, we will do the same with the human eye. We'll start by looking at its biological mechanisms and see how it's built. We'll see how it performs, what it captures and what it misses. The standard we'll return to is this: does the eye, like a camera, put a picture in your head that matches real things in the world?

Close encounters

Let's imagine we're aliens doing an autopsy on some poor truck driver beamed up in Kansas. We've done the basic probing and now want to figure out what those two jelly globes in the head are for.

If we pull out the eyeballs, we see they're connected to strings of tissue called optic nerves. We can follow the connections along these nerve tracts to see they lead into the brain. They cross over at the brain's base, what human neuroscientists call the optic chiasm. Looking in detail at the nerve tracts, we can see the signals from each eye have been merged before splitting again. After they cross, the two streams separate and go into two knee-shaped lumps within each side of the brain. These are called the lateral geniculate nuclei, which is Latin for 'knee-shaped lumps on the side', but sounds much more scientific.

The nerve tracts project to the back of the brain. As we trace the connections between individual cells, we see that the surface of the whole back lump of the brain receives input from the eyes; it's called the occipital lobe. Processing of visual stimuli dominates the surface of the brain: we are visual creatures by the measure of how much cerebral real estate we commit to it.

Signals from the eyes are processed in the occipital lobe in gradually more sophisticated ways, from recognising dots and lines, to edges and shapes. Information spreads from the back towards the front of the brain. One stream heads upwards across the brain's surface towards the top of the cortex, where it connects with motor systems that control action, doing things and locating them. Another stream heads out of the visual cortex around the sides towards the temporal lobe, just above the ears. This area of the brain is concerned with identifying, recognising and labelling things in the world.

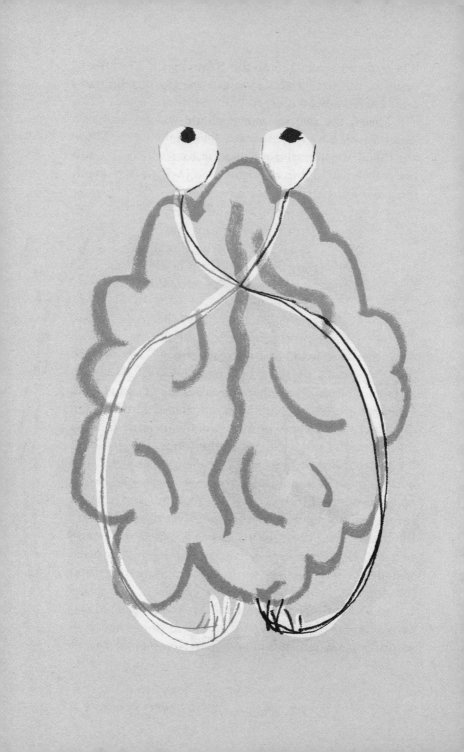

These two streams then project onwards to the frontal areas of the brain and to memory systems for short and long-term storage.

This is a vastly simplified picture of the 'bottom-up' information flow of the visual system, but it's good enough for our purpose, which is to see how much it resembles the wiring that might be inside your phone. That too works from a bottom-up flow of information, from sensors to processors. The signal from the light detectors is split and sent to various systems that might control the exposure, turn on the flash, or recognise faces and focus the image on them. The signals are then combined and recorded into long-term storage.

Why do pirates wear eye-patches?

Let's look more carefully at the eyeball. At the front there is a black circle, a hole called the pupil that lets in light. Just like an aperture on a film camera, it changes its size to let in light depending on external conditions. The pupil is a sphincter – a small ring of muscles. When you're gazing into your lover's eyes, you are gazing into their sphincters (I wouldn't point that out, though). It's worth seeing this muscle in action if you haven't noticed before. Stand very close to a mirror, close your eyes and count to thirty. Open your eyes and look at your pupils. You'll see them shrink.

The pupil also responds to cognitive effort and emotional arousal. If you're in love with something, your pupils widen. We recognise this response in others implicitly. It's why pupil sizes in advertisements are modified – so the model appears to be in love with her mid-range SUV. I think this is also why romantic dinners are candlelit. In response to low light levels, pupils widen. As this is the same response to feeling affection, and looks the same to other people, a candlelit dinner can be a way to encourage the signals of attraction.

Why do pirates wear eye patches? I had always assumed it was due to swashbuckling injuries, but this doesn't reflect reality. Records of the corpses of pirates don't appear to indicate a higher number of eye traumas, so why wear a patch over a healthy eye? One hypothesis is that it's to do with ship-to-ship combat. Pirates wear an eye patch while approaching another ship. They board with cutlasses ready. As they open the hatches to go below deck, there are sailors waiting for them in the dark. If a pirate leaps down the hatch, there will be several seconds while the pupils, adapted to the probably bright Caribbean sunshine, get used to the darkness, so the pirate will be blind and vulnerable to attack. To save those key seconds, they swap over the eye patch before jumping down and that pre-adapted eye will be ready to see through the gloom. We don't have direct proof of this, but it would certainly work as a tactic.

There are more camera-like features in the eyeball. There is a lens at the front which, rather than moving back and forth to focus, is squeezed by muscles to change its thickness to the same effect. Light passes into the eye through the pupil and lens and hits the back of the eyeball, called the retina. Just like a camera, this surface is coated in tiny sensors known as photoreceptors, which convert light energy into electrical signals. There are about 126 million of them of various types in the eye. Of particular interest are the cones, which we use for colour and fine-detail vision. There are about 6 million of those, which roughly corresponds to the number of image sensors you might find in a phone's camera.

In a digital camera, the sensors are arrayed in a neat, densely packed, uniform grid. That is not the case on the retina. There is one small spot, the fovea, in which the photoreceptor cells are so densely packed that the surface has buckled into a pit. Each area of the retina corresponds to a location in the visual field. The fovea is the spot right in the centre of your vision. It's tiny, just one per cent of the surface of your retina, and therefore it covers just one per cent of your visual field.

Stretch out your arm and stick up your thumb. Your fovea corresponds to the area of your thumbnail. Although it's small, the fovea is so densely packed with photoreceptors that half the information sent down your optic nerve comes from that area. Look at your thumbnail again: your brain is receiving as much visual information from that one-per-cent area as it is from the rest of your visual field put together.

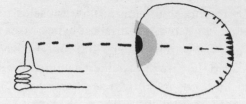

This huge disparity is nothing like your digital camera. You have as many image sensors attending to the bottom left of your camera's view as the centre. Your eye has fifty per cent of its information coming from one per cent of the area in the middle. In your peripheral vision outside the fovea you have very little detailed visual information at all. Peripheral vision is good at other things – low light and motion perception, in particular – but it is very poor at discriminating detail.

How can you perceive the world around you in detail when you can only really see out of one spot in the middle of your vision? You have to keep that spot moving all the time. A direct result of this disparity in detailed information is that your eyes move ceaselessly. You move your eyes about three or four times a second, shifting that high-accuracy fovea in high-speed movements called saccades, rooting out information. During the thirty milliseconds of these rapid movements, your brain shuts down the information feed to avoid a big smear of motion as the eye moves. In essence, you go momentarily blind for three or four times a second. You have to keep moving your eyes, though. In fact, if you were able to keep your eyes absolutely still they wouldn't work. Your eye is really only sensitive to changes in light stimulation, so needs constantly changing input. Even when you feel like you're keeping your eyes still, they are actually trembling slightly – in microsaccades – to keep themselves stimulated, much like a hyperactive toddler.

An intelligent design?

Imagine looking at a digital camera in a shop with the salesperson telling you it's a great camera, 6 million photoreceptors, but they're all bunched together in one spot in the middle and you have to move the camera three times a second or it stops working. That's actually a pretty poor camera.

The eye has bigger problems than temporary blindness, though. The photoreceptors in the retina are cells, and they need energy. Just like the image sensors in a camera are wired to the battery, eye cells need to be connected to a blood supply. The veins supplying the photoreceptors come off the surface of the retina into the eyeball, which causes a problem.

It's the same problem I had once when I repurposed an old cabinet into a media storage unit to hold my TV and satellite boxes. I wired them all together, then realised the power cables were inside the cabinet but needed to be plugged into the wall. After careful consideration, I took a hammer, bashed a hole in the back of the cabinet and ran the cables out. Job done.

It appears that someone with my appalling skills in planning and DIY has designed the eye. The veins that supply the retina cells simply exit the eyeball in a big hole at the back of the retina. Of course, where these cables go on the retinal surface, there can be no photoreceptors, so no vision. You are missing a chunk of your visual field that is about the size of a lemon held at arm's length. This is your blind spot. Usually, one eye can perceive the information in the other eye's blind spot. If you close one eye you don't find a big black hole in your vision. But it really is there – you are genuinely blind in that location, but your brain fills in the gap and gives you the sensation that you can see something. Your brain is bluffing.

If you were using a webcam, you might plug it into your laptop and look at the image on the screen while you move the camera around. Imagine our aliens doing something similar to an eye at the autopsy. The eye is pulled out of its socket and the dangling optic nerve is plugged into a computer. What would what's on the screen look like?

We actually know the answer because we know the properties of all those photoreceptors and can simulate their output on a computer. The image would be very blurry except for a tiny region in the centre. You'd have to move the camera three or four times a second, and each time you do, the image flickers out. There would be a big hole missing all the time, just off the centre. This is not a webcam you'd want, but we usually have two of them in our heads.

What's remarkable is that even though we have a poor-quality, uneven, constantly moving, shoddy visual input to the brain, what we experience is living in a richly detailed, stable and completely visual world. An experience that is an illusion generated by the brain. Like someone who turns up to a book club without having read the book, your brain is winging it, blithely claiming to know the story having only read the blurb on the back. We have far less perceptual information than we feel we do.

It's all an illusion

So far, we have examined the eye as alien scientists, comparing this messy suboptimal biological camera to a well-engineered digital camera. Now we should look at the eye's performance in the field. Although it seems to have a design that is less than perfect, the eye has evolved over forty times in history. On forty occasions, creatures with no common ancestors have separately evolved visual systems that share many of the characteristics of the human eye, such as a central fovea and the need for constant jerking motion. In contrast, no creature has a visual system that has a detailed uniform retina that gradually scans its environment like a CCTV camera. Biology most be doing something right.

But there are lots of occasions when the eye appears to make quite substantial errors. Pick up any book about visual illusions, for example, and you'll see images that appear to move and shift, lines that seem bent that are actually straight, objects that are different sizes but actually the same, colours and shadows where there are none.

Many of these are what we call 'bottom-up' illusions. They are produced by processing quirks in the early mechanisms of visual perception and passed up the line to higher levels of cognition. For example, although you have over 100 million photoreceptors in the back of the retina, there are only about one million cells in the optic nerve sending information to the brain. Why not send all the input from the retina to the brain? Well, if every photoreceptor sent a signal to the brain you would literally pass out from the metabolic effort of all the cell activity that would be needed to deal with the signal. The brain reduces the information sent down the optic nerve, and then again with the processing of early vision. This reduction comes in part from guesswork and shortcuts, which can be exploited in visual illusions.

Many errors in our visual system are quite familiar. Like a rundown car, we're used to living with its faults and quirks. I'm sure you have experienced after-images before, where you are exposed to a bright light such as a camera flash and can then see dots floating in front of your eyes. This is related to a feature of the visual system called adaptation. In certain circumstances, if a constant or intense stimulus is suddenly removed, an after-effect is produced.

My favourite demonstration of adaptation is the waterfall illusion. If you are next to a waterfall, or any stimulus with constant motion in a single direction, pick a point and stare at it without moving your eyes for thirty seconds or more. Then look away, or if you can, at the face of the person next to you. What you see is very hard to describe. You see the opposite motion – upwards, in the case of a waterfall – to that which you originally perceived. It's as if the world is melting and dripping upwards. At grad school, I saw people trying this out and screaming in horror as if on a bad mushroom trip. Actually, given where I went to grad school, it could have just been a bad mushroom trip.

Here's the thing that makes people gurgle in shock: nothing actually moves. You see motion, but without anything changing location, which is logically impossible. The person's face seems to melt upwards, but never leaves their head. What this tells us is that there is a part of the brain that codes for motion direction, gets fatigued and produces the after-effect, and that that part of the brain is separate from the part that codes for location. This is why you can experience something that is logically impossible.

The waterfall illusion also tells us that the brain uses population coding for motion. There are cells in your occipital lobe that fire when you see motion at a particular place, in a particular direction. To figure out the direction of motion for a particular place, the brain takes a vote across the population of brain cells for that location. Cells, like schoolchildren, are restless and get bored easily. In other words, they are rarely completely silent, but have a resting state of firing every once in a while. The only time that they go still is if they are fatigued. In the waterfall illusion, the cells coding for downwards motion get worn out. They run out of energy and stop firing completely. When the brain takes a population vote, the restless, base-rate firing of the cells coding for upwards motion beats the votes of the knackered, now-silent cells coding for downwards motion. Overall, you perceive upwards motion but without anything moving.

This form of adaptation – the brain reducing its response to constant stimuli – can be seen across the perceptual system. It is not something we would want in a digital camera. Looking back over my laptop's photo album, I calculated that when our first child was born

I took an average of one picture of him every forty minutes for the first two years of his life (such attention dropped off when his siblings were born, sadly for him). It would be no good if my camera was built to adapt to the constant stimulation of the fat, smiling face of my infant son and consequently blanked him in the pictures, or like in the waterfall illusion, hallucinated the opposite of him as a thin, screaming old man.

Seeing faces

The eye is not only plagued by bottom-up illusions stemming from its perceptual machinery. Just as cellular connections send data up from the sensor of the eye to the higher levels of cognition, there are also cells sending information in the opposite direction. Such higher levels – visual attention, object recognition and action control – send signals down to the lower levels that code for objects, lines and orientations. This design of the perceptual system produces another set of errors called 'top-down' illusions. What we perceive is not a function of what we see, but what we expect to see.

Our expectations about the world around us come from our experience of it. Top-down illusions are strongest for those things we experience the most. As human beings, one of the things we see most commonly are other humans, specifically their faces. For this reason, we have strong expectations about faces and tend to see them even when they are not there. Pareidolia is the term for this sort of hallucination, which is quite common. If you search online for pictures tagged with that word, you'll see Jesus in bits of toast, Elvis in wall mould, world leaders in the form of root vegetables and a series of houses that all look like Hitler. We have such strong expectations that, when exposed to mildly suggestive or ambiguous stimuli, we leap to the conclusion that there is a face looking at us.

The reason for top-down illusions can be seen in the connectivity of the brain. Remarkably, there are more connections coming down from higher levels of cognition than there are coming up from sensory mechanisms. Because of brain wiring, what you see is more of a function of what you expect to see than the data that is sent from your eyes.

Sleight of hand

We set out to evaluate the eye using the criteria of delivering an accurate internal representation of the external world. By this measure, when we line up the performance of the visual system with the performance of a camera, the eye seems to come off much worse. There might be good reasons for evolving a brain that quickly interprets and reacts to ambiguous stimuli on the basis of what it has experienced before, but it is the last thing you want in a camera. A camera should just record what is in front of it, not get bored with seeing some things and hallucinate what else it expects to see.

The eye is shaping up to function as a pretty poor camera, but we could also argue that the eye is just a messy biological system. Maybe it is striving to function as a camera, but our modern technology is simply more advanced. Let's examine human perception not in terms of its engineering or flaws, but its behaviour. Aside from visual illusions and mistaking bacon for Elvis, how does the perceptual system function in the real world? Does it deliver an internal representation of the world that, although imperfect, is good enough?

An experiment was done outside my office at Cornell University by Daniel Simons and Daniel Levin which has been repeated many times since (you can find the video on YouTube). In the scenario, it's the first week of classes and a new graduate student is lost. He approaches an elderly professor and asks for directions to the library. The professor replies, pointing at locations on a map and gesturing to buildings. Two men approach, carrying a door between them. Rudely, they march in between the student and the professor, blocking their view of each other. The student grabs the door and keeps walking with it. The second man grabs the map and takes the student's position. The student leaves, hidden by the door he carries. The second man and the professor are left facing each other. What do you think happens next?

The professor, looking at a completely new person to the one who began the conversation, just keeps talking. He doesn't miss a beat. He finishes the directions and bids the student (the man who had been carrying the door) goodbye.

Why didn't the professor stop to acknowledge that the student had changed from one person to another? Maybe he was so caught up in the task of giving directions that he never looked at the student's face. Perhaps he did notice, but didn't care that the face had changed, or put it down to some mushrooms he took the other day while watching a waterfall.

Each of these hypotheses we can test, but each of them fails to explain the phenomenon now known as 'change blindness'. With eye-tracking devices we can show that during experiments such as the one above, people will look directly at the faces before and after they change. We can ask them afterwards if they noticed anything but were too embarrassed to say, but they usually have no clue. We can also test them for mushrooms.

A remaining possibility is that the professor was perhaps too engaged in the task of giving directions and simply did not expect a shape-shifting undergraduate. We can test that hypothesis in a much simpler version of the experiment – one that you can take part in. I've set this up based on the work of Ron Rensink, a pioneer in this field. Go to this page: http://eyethink.org/changeblind and follow the instructions.

In the experiment, you are being asked to look for a single change between two similar images flicking back and forth. It is your only task. You're not giving directions to a stranger at the same time. It's only two images, not a complex social interaction. This should be easy, right?

Many people struggle to see the change right in front of their eyes. The first surprising thing is that it takes a lot of people a good few moments – even a minute or more – to see it. The second surprising thing is that once you've seen the change, you can't not see it, it's that obvious. If a person couldn't see it, you'd think they had brain damage. At the start of the experiment, you were that person.

We have shown – in the lab and in real life – that if a large change occurs in the visual world, as long as the moment of the change is hidden by a sleight of hand such as the door intrusion, most people simply won't notice – around sixty per cent, in fact. That anyone at all should miss such an obvious change is remarkable.

Change blindness can be shown in many ways. With sleight of hand when a switch happens behind a door, with a tiny flicker between altered photographs, or even just with an event that momentarily distracts you. As long as the moment of the change is out of immediate sight, it is remarkably hard for people to spot it. It seems

as if we simply don't remember many of the details of the world around us.

I was once lecturing at Stanford University about change blindness and might have gently teased the students for not being able to spot the changes, even though they were allegedly the smartest in the country. The next week, I was lecturing about language processing. It was a hot day and a slightly long-winded talk. At the end, I asked if there were any questions. There was the usual awkward silence, then someone asked, 'Have you noticed anything?' I shrugged, imagining they had spotted a minor grammatical error on one of the slides. Then, suddenly, everyone in the room was wearing white. Pure white T-shirts. All staring at me. It wasn't a sudden change. No one had moved, they had been there all the time. It was one of the more bizarre and alarming moments of my life.

It turns out the students had hatched a plot after my joking in the change blindness lecture. They told everyone to wear a white T-shirt under a sweater that day, then followed a simple rule while I was lecturing: if a student couldn't see anyone else moving, then they were to slowly take off their sweater. This is why it had struck me that it was a hot day, as I'd noticed people were peeling off layers. However, the change was gradual enough that I never noticed what they were wearing underneath until that gut-wrenching moment when I suddenly saw it. It was apt revenge.

Change blindness is perhaps the biggest failure of the visual system when we compare it to a camera. A computer could tell in an instant that the two images in the online experiment were different. A CCTV camera could easily record that the person asking for directions had changed, or that a room full of people had changed into white T-shirts.

The system works

It's not just that the eye stores a poor internal representation of the external world; it's that the visual system barely seems to be trying to store these representations at all. It's not just that the visual system functions as a bad camera and storage device, either. It's that it seems to have a different function entirely. That is why a camera is a poor metaphor for the eye.

If not to record the world around us, what is the function of the visual system? It seems it helps us to *do* things, to be active in the world rather than to passively and faithfully record it. And to do that it has evolved functions that look like lazy shortcuts when compared to a digital camera. One is to use what is called external memory, to use the world as its own best representation. Rather than memorise, for example, the face of an undergraduate asking for directions, your visual system

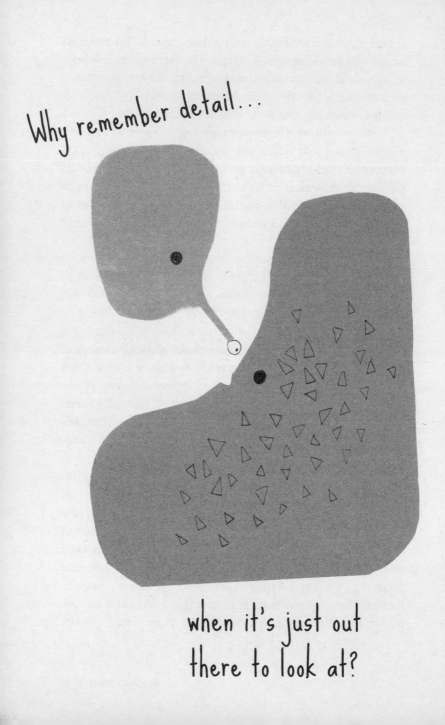

relies on the fact that if you need to know what he looks like at any point, you can just move your eyes to his face. Your visual system assumes the information is out there, so why bother to encode and store it?

Eye-tracking work by Dana Ballard, Mary Hayhoe and others shows that when people are asked to copy a complete LEGO model with a pile of bricks, they continually look back at the model. They could memorise it all in one look, but it's more efficient for the visual system to leave the information out there and fixate it again with a glance. Indeed, if you sneakily change the brick colours during those thirty milliseconds when they move their eyes and are blind, people do not notice at all. They blissfully continue to build, showing that they never memorise the block colours. Work in my own lab shows that if you are trying to recall a fact once told to you by a face on a computer screen, your gaze will return to that empty location on the screen. For your visual system, knowing something is less a case of storing information as being able to find it again.

This reliance on external memory usually works without a hitch. People rarely change their faces mid-sentence, objects don't disappear in thirty milliseconds and undergraduates hardly ever engage in choreographed costume changes. The system generally works. It is only when an experimenter (or smug students) make a change exactly at the right moment, in exactly the right way, that external memory breaks down. It's an efficient way for the visual system to guide behaviour, but it makes for a very poor camera.

Sight vs man

Right now, you have very little knowledge of many of the visual details around you. The evidence from eye anatomy suggests that, outside of the little spot of your fovea, you have very little incoming information about what's happening near you. The evidence from change blindness suggests that if I had the magical means, I could change the outfit of a person in the room with you, the colour of the wallpaper, maybe even your own shoes, and you'd have no idea. The amazing thing is that you *feel* you know what the world around you looks like. It seems as if you have an accurate internal representation of your external world. However, that's an illusion. Just like your brain fills in that black hole of your retinal blind spot, it also blithely gives the impression that you have reliable stored knowledge of the world around you. When we think of visual illusions, we think of lines that look like they're different lengths but are actually the same size, or things that look wobbly but aren't. They are nothing. The biggest visual illusion of them all is that, despite what you feel, you don't have any richly detailed idea of what is going on around you.

You have little idea
what is going on
around you right now

Mind vs opinion

How do people try to change our minds?

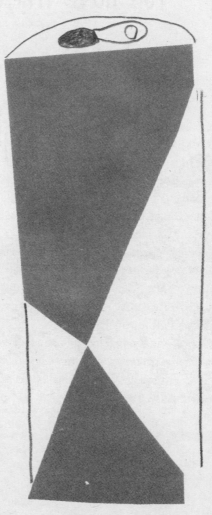

The premise of an enlightened democracy, with its open debate and discussion, is that people can change their minds. That principle is built into any legal system that relies on deliberation, and methods of teaching through debate that go back to the ancient Greeks. The third act of most dramas involves a character who is persuaded by another's argument to join a fight, become a hero or take the high road. So what are the real psychological processes of a dramatic volte-face? Which arguments work and what appeals to reason? How do pre-existing beliefs and emotions pull people one way or another? How do you change a mind?

Psychological evidence gives a powerful insight into what actually governs our debates and decisions, and provides an answer to one of the enduring mysteries of our age: why the hell does anyone buy energy drinks?

The facts speak for themselves

'Rhetoric is the art of ruling the minds of men,' wrote the ancient Greek philosopher Plato. The way to change the hearts and minds of men is through finely tuned, elegant argumentation. But 2016 was not a good year for rhetoric. The soaring cadences and stirring speeches of President Obama gave way to the rambling, narcissistic tweets of President-elect Trump.

According to most polls, Trump had lost the presidential debates by a wide margin. In his speeches, he made objectively false statements at a rate of over one per minute. The fact-checking website PolitiFact rated his statements against objective, verifiable facts and found that seventy per cent of every statement he made was somewhere between 'mostly false' and the site's highest rating, 'pants on fire'. Despite his brutish manner of speech and bleak dishonesty, Trump won the election. He successfully changed minds.

As well as the power of rhetoric, the ancient Greeks believed in many strange things: that flies grew spontaneously from rotten meat, sheep could grow on trees and women had fewer teeth than men. The advantage of the scientific revolution is that we stopped believing people just because they were ancient and Greek. *Nullius in verba* – take no one's word for it – as the motto of the Royal Society goes. Instead of repeating the words of revered men with beards, we can observe the world, find the fly eggs and bother to count women's teeth. Perhaps a belief in the lofty Greek art of rhetoric has gone the same way. In our information-rich age, maybe we are less persuaded by artfully mannered speechifying and driven instead by 'hard facts'.

Here are some stats for you to digest. In Indonesia, sea levels were measured in 1996 across several locations. That year, there were 669 places with an increase in sea levels, and 225 places with a decrease. In 2016, another set of measurements was taken across another set of locations. In that year, 321 places saw an increase, and 63 had a decrease. Does this data suggest that sea levels have been generally rising from 1996 to 2016?

Here's a second data set to process. In some American cities, it is legal to carry a concealed handgun. Last year, crime decreased in 107 of those cities, and increased in 21. Some cities introduced a ban on handguns, and crime decreased in 223 of those cities and increased in 75. From these data, is crime lower when people can legally carry concealed weapons, or is crime lower when they have been banned?

Do you have your answers? There are three important things to point out. Firstly, I made up these data. Well, I adapted them from the work of law professor Dan Kahan and his colleagues, but they are not real data. Secondly, I'm guessing that, like most people who answer these questions in the UK, you said yes to the first question and no to the second. You concluded that climate change is real and gun control reduces crime. Thirdly, you're wrong. That's not what the data say.

The maths behind these questions is pretty easy. To interpret the data, you just need to calculate ratios – to do the sort of division you were probably doing at school. In the sea level data set, we can see that the 1996 increases in sea levels outnumber decreases by about 3 to 1. In 2016, increases outnumber decreases by 5 to 1. The data say that increases are more common in 2016. This is the one you got right because the odds are that you are neither a moron who rejects climate change, nor paid directly by the oil industry to deny it.

What about the second question? The second data set actually has near identical ratios. In cities with legally concealed handguns, crime decreases outnumber increases by about 5 to 1. In cities that introduced a ban on handguns, decreases outnumber increases only by about 3 to 1. Therefore, the ban is relatively bad for crime rates. You probably got this question wrong. If so, I'd guess that you aren't a fervent believer in the right to bear arms and think that having guns in society is a bad thing for crime. It's this pre-existing belief in favour of gun control that made you misinterpret the plain facts in front of you because they went against your narrative.

Even though the two questions on climate change and gun control are identical in their mathematical structure and difficulty, people fail the second when they are pro-gun control. Just to be clear, this is not one of those demonstrations about how bad people are at everyday maths. That's not the point. You are probably well able to make these calculations and get the right answer. Unless, of course, the answer conflicts with an opinion or belief of your own, which *is* the point.

Researchers showed these questions to American Democratic and Republican voters with varying levels of maths education. They created two versions, with the numbers switched around. People got the answer wrong whenever the numbers they were looking at went against their political beliefs, just as you might have. Remarkably, they were more likely to make this error the higher their level of maths education. That seems completely backwards, but I ran this experiment myself with people at an event for scientists and science documentary makers in London. These people, who had very successful careers collecting, interpreting and explaining scientific data, screwed up a basic question of division.

One explanation is that if you have an opinion and you feel it is grounded in facts, then you simply don't bother to calculate the ratios and go with your hunch. If you are mathematically literate and think you know the numbers, then you are more likely to go with a hunch about the right answer and completely fail to see what the numbers actually say. The scientists behind this particular demonstration call it 'motivated numeracy', which is a nice phrase. The whole point about numbers and scientific data is that they don't care about who you are or what you believe. Of course, people can lie and fudge the truth with selective statistics, but that's not what is going on in these demonstrations. The numbers clearly do support one answer, but we fail to reach that conclusion if it disagrees with our pre-existing view. Opinion trumps fact.

My way or the highway

How common is this problem? I said that it mostly occurs when you feel that your opinion is grounded in facts. That just happens to be all of the time. This is called 'naive realism' and it is one of those biases in our thinking that is so broad and ever-present that it's hard to even notice it is there.

The bias is that we have a tendency to confuse our subjective opinion with objective reality. For example, I've used exclusively Apple computers for about twenty years. I get an allergic reaction whenever I have to interact with a PC and its clunky, backwards operating system. Abstractly, I know this is just an opinion, and that if I had used a PC as my first computer I probably would have got used to it, ended up preferring Windows and finding Macs odd and alien. That feels wrong even to type out. I want to say that it's not merely my opinion that Macs are better, they're just better machines. This slide from personal opinion to believed fact, is the essence of naive realism.

A consequence of naive realism is that if people have a different opinion to us, there is only one explanation: they must be factually wrong. My thinking is based in fact, and if you disagree with me then your opinion must be a result of bias or error. If you want further illustration of this, just read the comments section of any internet page. From debates about government surveillance to the best episodes of *Buffy the Vampire Slayer*, 'I guess we just have different viewpoints on the issue' is a much less common comment than, 'That's how the Nazis started'.

This bias is extremely hard to shift. A psychology professor asked his students to define naive realism on a multiple-choice exam. Most correctly picked, 'confusing subjective opinion with objective reality'. In a follow-up question, he asked about who is susceptible to this bias. Most chose the answer, 'other people, but not me'. In other words, they made the error of naive realism in the course of answering a question about it.

The best job in the world

How do we change people's minds when they are so entrenched and conflate fact and opinion? Let's dig down to examine the motivations that people have for holding a set of beliefs or choosing a course of action.

This is the story of an experiment published in a high-profile journal that got lots of media attention. It all began when my old friend, developmental psychologist Steve Mock, rang the doorbell of our house in California. When I opened the door to Steve, the man he saw was not the person he knew from grad school. I had not slept in four weeks and was wearing sweatpants backwards. I had vomit on one sleeve and snot down my front. I had a newborn baby under one arm and her twin brother under the other. Steve, dressed immaculately as always, walked in. I think it was at that moment that the question of why people ever want to have children struck him. Not every parent was as hapless as I appeared in that moment, but when people are surveyed, those with children seem less happy, have less marital satisfaction and are more prone to clinical depression. So why do parents do it?

Later, after feeding me, helping with the kids and generally making life easier, Steve returned to his university and began a project with his colleague Richard Eibach. They asked people with children a series of questions about how important being a parent was to them, how much they enjoyed time with their offspring, how much time they intended to spend with their kids that coming weekend, and so on. Before answering, the parents were given some information. One set of parents was informed, quite correctly, that the average cost of raising a child to the age of sixteen in the US was about $200,000. That's before paying for college or a wedding, or helping out with a house. The second set of parents was told of this cost, but also of one of the benefits: elderly people tend to be happier and healthier in their lives if they have had children. In purely selfish terms, it pays to have children and grandchildren when you are old. Another group of parents wasn't told either of these costs or benefits.

So who likes being a parent more? The people who have just been told that each kid costs them two-hundred grand, or the people who were told the cost and also the benefit that they bring in the long term?

The only rational answer is the second one. If you could invest in a property that cost $200,000 and then disappeared, or one that cost the same but you could sell for a profit afterwards, surely the one with the benefits looks better? Of course, being a parent is nothing like a financial investment, and there are many other factors and emotions involved. However, since all those factors would be the same for the parents in the two groups with information, then it's rational to think that the parents told of the benefits to being a parent would be the ones who felt better about it.

That is not what Mock and Eibach found. The parents reminded only of the enormous financial cost of being a parent were more likely to say that being a parent was really special to them, that it was the most valuable thing in their lives, that they loved every moment they spent with their kids and would take the whole weekend to spend time with them. Why did these parents' love for their kids increase with knowledge of their cost and decrease with the benefits? Why are people backwards in their reasoning?

If I asked to you list basic human needs, you might list things such as food, water and shelter, or perhaps love, belonging and truth, or maybe good wifi. However, we have another need that is remarkably underappreciated and would not occur to many people. We need to feel consistent. We have to make sense, at least to ourselves. The feeling that our thoughts and actions don't make sense, that there is a contradiction or inconsistency between them, is called 'cognitive dissonance'. It explains why thinking about being penniless increases the love that parents feel for their children and so much else besides.

Cognitive dissonance is an unpleasant feeling. We are motivated to remove the dissonance, like scratching an itch. How do you remove contradictions between your beliefs and actions? Well, you change your beliefs, think up new ones and act in a different way until things make sense.

Consider the parents who are told of the costs of having their children. Thinking about that huge amount of money might produce dissonance. Who spends $200,000 on something? What could be worth that amount? There's a way that the cost is justified: the parents must really love their kids. Really, really love them. Being a parent must be the most important thing to them, since it's obviously the most expensive thing they've ever done. Increasing the love they feel for their children justifies those costs. It makes sense and scratches the itch.

The parents who are told about the benefits of having children do not experience dissonance in this way. To be sure, the costs are there, but they have a justification for them: kids make your life better when you are older. In that light, the costs make sense. There is no dissonance to explain away, so those parents are less likely to say that being a parent is as important to them and less likely to idealise parenthood.

Drinking the Kool Aid

Mock and Eibach did not invent the theory of cognitive dissonance, although the parental idealisation study is a very nice application of the theory. It comes from the work of social psychologist Leon Festinger in the 1950s.

Festinger came to the notion of cognitive dissonance following his studies of cults. He was fascinated with doomsday cults who believed in prophecies that the end of the world is nigh. Such groups have cropped up many times in history, particularly when the calendar reaches some significant date. They were common at the turn of the previous two millennia, and more recently in 2012, which some thought marked the end of the Mayan calendar. Festinger was particularly interested in what happened the day after whatever was supposed to happen had not happened – the doomsday, the ascension of the cult members, or the arrival of the mother ship. In that moment, Festinger wondered what the cult members felt about their beliefs. Was there any sense of anger, shame or rejection? The psychologist and his colleagues joined a cult under false names to find out.

They realised that cultists were more likely to strengthen their devotion to a cult following a failed prophecy. Again, this seems backwards. In the face of strong counterevidence, people believed even more. Why didn't they change their minds? It seems irrational if people are motivated by truth and accuracy and evidence. But it turned out they weren't. The day the prophecy failed, the cultists would be feeling a contradiction between their situation – no angels, aliens or Armageddon – and all their beliefs in the prophecy. The problem is, if they rejected those beliefs, there

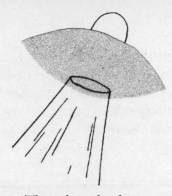

would be yet more dissonance. They thought they were rational, sensible people, but if they rejected the cult, they would have to admit that they had been duped, that they had wasted their time and money and cut off their friends and family for no reason. This would produce overwhelming dissonance.

So what is the best way out of this mess of contradictions? How can the cult members' actions and beliefs be justified? The shortest route would be to believe that the cult teachings are right and they are good and sensible people who were correct to trust their prophet. Maybe the leader added up the ages of Noah's wives incorrectly, or had the wrong translation of the Mayan runes. Perhaps the aliens decided we weren't ready and would return in ten years. Time and time again in the history of failed prophecies, cult members discover a reason to explain how things didn't quite happen as expected, but really, really would any time soon. That's not to say people don't make the decision to leave cults for lots of reasons, but the point is that dramatic, incontrovertible contradictions of core beliefs don't tend to provoke departures. Faith is unharmed, and indeed strengthened, by the biggest failure of those beliefs.

Christianity itself began exactly in this way, with a group of people who believed that Jesus' return was not an abstract future event, but that he would return in their lifetimes. He didn't, and I think it is possible to see much of the changes in the early doctrine of Christianity as shifts in belief generated by the cognitive dissonance of this absence.

No pain, no gain

Festinger was a wonderful scientist because he followed his studies of cultists with careful experiments in the lab. In a classic study, he asked participants to do a boring task for an hour, turning pegs by ninety degrees over and over. Afterwards, Festinger asked each participant to tell the next person that it was actually a fun study. It really wasn't, but most did as asked and told the lie. He then gave them $1 or $20 for taking part. Finally, he asked his key question: despite what they said to the person in the waiting room, did they actually enjoy the experiment?

The participants might have been feeling dissonance at this point. They had just lied after all, telling a stranger that it was fun. Good people don't lie like that. However, the person paid $20 had a justification for their actions. This experiment took place in the 1950s, so that $20 is worth about £80 now – plenty of justification to tell a little white lie. Those participants said that the experiment was indeed pretty dull. The participants paid $1 had a problem. They had no adequate justification for their lie. They felt cognitive dissonance. How could they reduce it? Those participants told Festinger – and themselves – that they did quite enjoy the experiment.

Whenever there is insufficient reward, there will be dissonance. It can be removed if people change their minds about their beliefs and attitudes. As Festinger put it, 'people will come to value and love that which they suffer for'.

This obviously seems like nonsense. Our complete understanding of the world is that people love and value that for which they are rewarded. They work harder for those rewards because they value those things. That's why we offer people more money for jobs of greater value and why we reward our children with praise and presents for good behaviour. Those sentiments are rational, but psychologically they are wrong. If you ask people which jobs they value, it is not those that pay more. Nurses, who work for a lower wage, will typically value their work more than a banker with a yacht-sized bonus. Indeed, nurses are more likely to feel that they have a vocation *because* of that low wage. They 'love that which they suffer for'. In relationships, this is the sad scientific evidence behind the cruel phrase, 'treat 'em mean, keep 'em keen'.

American university fraternities have a period of 'hazing', where potential new recruits have to pass through a series of degrading and painful tests. If Brad eventually tells them they are now part of the brotherhood, what do they think about him and the fraternity? What do they think of the man who made them streak across a quad wearing a moose's head, put his three-day-old gym socks in their mouth and drink what might have been his pee? How do they cope with the dissonance of degrading themselves? Well, Brad must be a pretty awesome guy and this fraternity deserves lifelong loyalty – that's the only way to justify the suffering and remove the dissonance. Again, completely counter-intuitively, the degree of humiliation caused by a fraternity serves only to increase the love and devotion it receives.

The art of selling

People have a need for meaning and consistency that swamps their need for truth, accuracy or even happiness. If that's true, how can we ever hope to change people's minds? It seems that we can't use facts if they run counter to beliefs. We can't use reason and reward if it risks disrupting the delicate balance of self-justification. The need for consistency – stubbornness that can ignore facts such as a failed prophecy – is just too strong. Using the psychological judo of persuasion techniques, however, the strength of cognitive dissonance can be used against someone to change their mind.

In for a pound

In for a penny

If you walked up to someone in the street and asked for a monthly £10 direct debit for a homeless charity, you'd be likely to collect few donations. If you tried the 'foot-in-the-door' technique, you might get a different result. Asking someone, 'Do you have thirty seconds to talk about homelessness?' seems like a small commitment for such an important topic and people would stop to talk. After a chat, you could ask them to sign a petition to the local council asking for more help for the homeless. Then you can ask for the direct debit. Watch the money come in.

The point here is that people's need to feel consistent is exploited by the chuggers who stop people on the street. They don't really want to chat or collect your signature – these small requests are only made so you'll act consistently and say yes when they make the bigger request for money.

Another version of this sneaky technique is the 'bait and switch', as used by some salespeople. They advertise a really good deal for, say, a new phone. You make the trip to the shop to snap one up, but the phone is out of stock, or they don't have the model you wanted. The bait has gone. However, there is another one that is very similar, just a little more expensive. That's the switch. What salespeople find is that people will buy the second phone offered, even if it no longer offers very good value. People have already engaged in all the required behaviours – leaving the house, turning up at the shop with their money, talking to the salesperson – so it would seem inconsistent to refuse a deal for a phone.

The simplest way to exploit the need for consistency is just to tell people what to think. It's called labelling. You walk into a car dealership and have a peer around.

The salesperson asks you what you're looking for. You mumble something about hybrid cars and performance. They seize on this like you're Jeremy Clarkson and tell you that you definitely know what you're talking about, and so on. You may have thought it was just aimless flattery, but they are specifically ascribing traits to you that describe someone who would spend more money on a car. When the moment comes and you have to decide whether to go for the GL or XXL Deluxe model you think, 'Yeah, I appreciate quality.'

Are you sure?

Perhaps this sounds implausible. Can people really be duped so easily? Can you change someone's mind about what car they would buy just by telling them they're a big spender? Surely people have a better sense of themselves and could resist these labels? It turns out that evidence for that premise is surprisingly weak. We know ourselves and our own choices quite poorly.

In one of my favourite experiments, researchers Petter Johansson and Lars Hall showed participants two photographs of people they might like to date. The participant pointed to whichever one they found more attractive, in a sort of analogue version of Tinder. The researcher put the cards down, then picked up the one that the participant had pointed to. They asked the person to explain in more detail why they made that choice and what they found attractive, to give the person on the card a mark out of ten, etc. This was done several times.

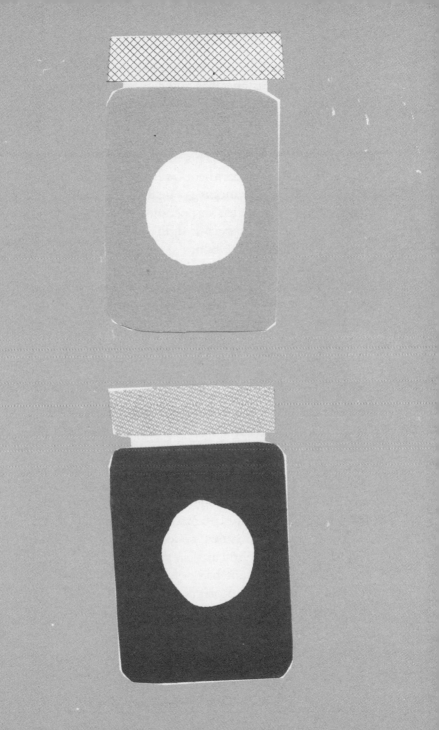

Sometimes, the researcher would use some sleight of hand while he put the cards down, a bit like a magician. What they would actually show to the participant for discussion was not the person they chose, but the person they didn't choose. Amazingly, participants often didn't notice the switch. This might remind you of the change blindness experiments we discussed in chapter two, but these experiments go further. The researchers then looked at the reasons people gave for choosing one person from the pair. It didn't matter whether the participant was talking about the face they chose, or the face that they didn't choose: the reasons for their choice, their ratings and their certainty were all the same. This is remarkable. Even if people didn't notice the change, you'd expect their ratings and evaluations of the people they chose to be higher and better than their evaluations of the people they didn't choose – because, well, they didn't choose them.

It works for jam, too. In a real supermarket, the researchers gave shoppers two different jams to taste. They asked them to point to their preference, gave them another taste, then asked them to give reasons for their choice. There was another sleight of hand as the researchers turned the jars upside-down and switched the flavours between tastings. They found that shoppers who had moments ago pointed to one flavour as their preference would then take a second taste (of the other flavour) and confidently explain the reason for their first choice, despite the switch.

And it works for politics. During a local election in Sweden, the researchers surveyed people on their attitudes. In one example, they asked them to place a cross on a line to indicate how concerned they were about immigration. Watching how the participant was answering, the researcher was filling in another survey, copying their responses and the style of their X's, but putting down the opposite of their answers. When the participant had finished, they took the survey, covered it with the inverted one, and asked the participant to talk through some of the issues. They asked questions about why the participant was concerned about immigration, and so on. Often, the participant would respond with detailed reasons for the exact opposite opinion to the one that they just declared to be their own.

This is known as 'choice blindness'. It suggests a surprising answer to the question of how to change someone's mind: you just tell them what they think and they will happily go along with it. One explanation for this phenomenon is that, as change blindness shows, you encode surprisingly little of the world around you, including your own behaviour. Your fragile memory can apparently be swamped by a researcher holding one card that apparently you chose, or showing you a survey with what looks like your cross on it. Faced with this evidence, your need for consistency drives you to confabulate perfectly sincere reasons for choosing a face or being worried about immigrants.

The sort of blatant trickery in these choice blindness experiments rarely happens in everyday life. However, salespeople and politicians often try to change minds by telling people what they think. From labelling potential clients as 'platinum customers', to making statements such as 'the British people are tired of being in Europe', one of the most powerful ways to change minds is to tell people that they have already changed.

Opinion vs man

We think of persuasion as the first step to changing behaviour. You have to capture hearts and minds to bring change to people's actions. Psychological science suggests that is this backwards. Beliefs and attitudes are not the root cause of behaviour. The phenomenon of cognitive dissonance shows that beliefs can be reshuffled and switched in retrospect to make sense of behaviour. You make someone lie about enjoying an experiment and they decide that they had fun after all. You make someone suffer to be a part of your club and they want it even more because of that suffering. You reward them less and they like it more.

None of this remotely matches the simple model of human behaviour that is commonly used by economists or marketing people. They assume we work harder for rewards and value things that make us happy. Psychologically, that is not a valid assumption, but if you realise how to exploit these strange features of our psychology you can use them to great effect.

Take Red Bull, the energy drink. It tastes disgusting, comes in a can that is smaller than its rivals and is more expensive. Imagine pitching that idea to your sales team: it's new, it's gross, it's small, it's pricey! But it would seem that someone on Red Bull's sales team had taken a psychology class. I think they designed a drink specifically with those negative attributes so its consumers would wonder why they had paid so much for a tiny drink that tastes like a robot's pee, justify their behaviour and come to love it, believing that it must be potent and giving them so much energy. People came to value that which they suffered for, and Red Bull became the fastest-growing drink in the market since Coca-Cola. Understand that and you will change people's minds.

Mind vs colour

Do we see the same blue?

'Zeus had blasted and shattered his swift ship with a bright lightning bolt, out on the wine-dark sea.'

William Gladstone, a classicist (and four-time British prime minister), was obsessed by these lines written by the ancient Greek poet Homer. 'Wine-dark sea'? What could that mean? At night, the sea could be as dark as a glass of Merlot, or perhaps the sea was thick with the blood of warriors. However, in this case the action happens during the day and there has been no bloodshed. More puzzlingly, Homer describes oxen as 'wine-looking', the sky is often compared to bronze and honey, and the faces of angry men are likened to green things such as grass. These might be explained as poetic licence, but when Gladstone looked though all of Homer's work for his book *Studies on Homer and the Homeric Age*, he found something quite strange. References to black and white were very common, as were violet, red and yellow. However, there was only one green – and there was no blue.

Was Homer colour-blind? We will never know for sure, as we know almost nothing about Homer the person, aside from some mostly discredited stories. In fact, Homer might even be the collected work of a whole culture of ancient Greeks, later attributed to a sagacious man with a beard. Even if Homer was a solitary, colour-blind genius, it seems remarkable that no one writing down or passing on his stories thought to correct his colour errors, if that's what they were. Perhaps all ancient Greeks were colour-blind? This appears to be Gladstone's conclusion when he writes, 'the organ of colour and its impressions were but partially developed among the Greeks of the heroic age'.

How could you ever know that another person sees the same colours as you? This question arose more recently in 2015 in an online meme. Someone had taken a picture of a dress in a shop that was clearly white and gold to some people, but clearly blue and black to others. The image was widely publicised, dividing friends and families. At some point in discussing such issues, someone will ask if we all *really* see the same colours. To answer the question in this chapter, we have to talk about the transduction of light into nerve signals in the eye, human mutant interior decorators and mantis shrimps. Which will all lead us back to that dress.

BLUE

blue

Time-travelling Homer

blue

Science is all about asking the right questions. So before we delve into data, let's think about how we could go about scientifically testing what colours people experience. Let's imagine we have transported Homer from ancient Greece to the modern world for a disorientating set of experiments.

To start with, we'll give Homer a glass of red wine and show him some pictures of the seaside. The first test is to see if he uses the same word to describe both, as his poetry suggests. As anyone who has bought paint will know, there is a difference between using the word for something and being able see the difference. Dulux sells a hundred colours in what I would call 'yellow', but if you were to paint your house with different pots, you'd see a mess of magnolia, corn yellow and sunrise beige. Perhaps we can give some paint swatches to Homer and ask him to put together the ones that show the same colours. This is a test not of the words he uses, but of the colours he sees. We might find that he sorts the swatches in the same way as us, or colour-blindly lumps all the blues and reds together.

However, even if Homer does sort the swatches in the same way as us, does he *really* see the same blue? His sorting behaviour might be identical to ours, but what does he actually *experience* in his head? Rather than italicising words all the time, philosophers have invented a word for this internal experience or sensation: the quale. My quale of blue is the phenomenology of the colour, the thing that I – and only I – experience. How do I know that my quale, my blue, is the same as Homer's or yours?

We can try performing a thought experiment, as philosophers (too lazy to do actual experiments) often do. Imagine that when you were born, an evil scientist attached special contact lenses to your eyeballs that had the effect of inverting the wavelengths of light in the visible colour spectrum. (Could a contact lens do this? Not really, but philosophers don't get hung up on such details.) Light of 420 nanometres in length, which most of us perceive as blue, gets stretched out to 700 nanometres, which most of us perceive as red, and vice versa.

These contact lenses never leave your eyes, staying there as you go to school, learn the words for colours, eat crayons and eventually find yourself in the paint aisle choosing colours. Since you consistently experience light at a wavelength of 700 nanometres that the rest of us are experiencing at 420 nanometres, and learned that the word 'blue' was the name for that colour, you would call the same things blue as everyone else. At the paint shop you would have the same success naming, sorting, picking your colours and agreeing with others what shade and hue they were. However, despite passing the naming test and the sorting swatches test exactly the same as everyone else, in this thought experiment we know that what you experience inside, your quale, is completely different to everyone else.

These thought experiments – time-travelling Homer and the evil sight-altering optometrist – can't answer our scientific questions about blue, but they do show us what we have to explain. In sketching out these experiments we will discuss colour perception in the eye, linguistic labels that people use for colours, how these colour terms are learned, how they might differ between languages, how colours are sorted non-linguistically, and what people experience when they observe colours.

Paint a rainbow

Let's start with the rainbow and the physiological process of colour perception. How many colours are there in a rainbow? Most people would probably say seven, naming them as red, orange, yellow, green, blue, indigo and violet. It's the wrong answer. The number of colours and the colours named are both incorrect – your teacher lied to you.

There aren't seven colours in a rainbow, not really. If a child drew a rainbow, they might pick out seven crayons from the box, but when you look at a rainbow what you are seeing are wavelengths of light that are continuously changing, from around 400 to around 800 nanometres: the visible spectrum of light. If you were to plot the physical waves of light across a rainbow, it would be a straight line of gradually increasing lengths. What we perceive doesn't look like a gradual change, it looks like solid bands of colour that overlap and merge a bit. If we were to plot what we *perceive*, it would be more like a staircase, with a band of red that transitions to a band of yellow, and so on. The fact that we see bands of colour is an outcome of the physiology of our eyes. When a child picks a set of seven crayons to draw a rainbow, they may not be representing the physics of the rainbow properly, but they are drawing what they *see*.

The child is still wrong, though. Why did they choose seven colours? Why are we taught that there are precisely seven named colours in a rainbow? Is it a feature of eye physiology or linguistic labels that make us see seven colours? The answer is that the seventeenth-century scientist Sir Isaac Newton decided himself that there were seven colours and we have stuck with his answer ever since. Why? Well, seven is a nice number.

Newton is a fascinating man. We typically think of him as one of the founding fathers of modern science, but as the economist John Maynard Keynes put it, 'Newton was not the first of the age of reason, he was the last of the magicians'. Less well known than his work in mathematics and physics are his voluminous and earnest writings on the occult, alchemy and numerology. It turns out that Newton was a bit of a nut. These two aspects of his character came together when he first split white light into a spectrum of colour using a glass prism. He provided a wonderful scientific and mathematical description of the phenomenon, then had to describe how many colours were in this continually changing rainbow. Given that Newton was obsessed by numerology, and since there are seven notes in the musical chromatic scale, he decided there should be seven colours in the rainbow. It's just how he thought it should be.

The final colour typically drawn in a rainbow is purple. This is what you get when you mix blue and red. However, in a rainbow the bands of colour go from red at the top to blue at the bottom. In other words, the red and blue never mix – they don't touch in a real rainbow. You have never seen a purple band in a rainbow. You might have seen one in a drawing, but it shouldn't be there. It's another lie.

Let's focus on the physiology of the eye and how it responds to these different wavelengths of light. At the back of your eyeball are cells that perform this magic step of transduction – changing photons of light into impulses of nerve energy. There are two types of these photoreceptors. Rods detect low levels of dim, blueish light and are not heavily involved in colour perception.

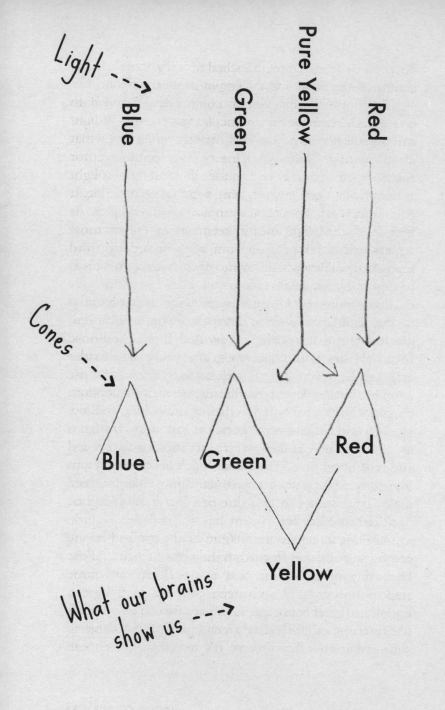

Light - - - >

Blue   Green   Pure Yellow   Red

Cones - - - >

Blue   Green   Red

Yellow

What our brains
show us - - - >

We're focusing on cones, bunched up very densely in the centre of your vision and doing most of the work.

There are three types of cone. Each is tuned to give a peak response to a particular wavelength of light and gives a response that tails off for wavelengths that are increasingly different. One type of photoreceptor sends its strongest nerve impulses when it detects light at roughly 445 nanometres (nm), which is a deep blue. It gives a weaker response to cyan and greenish blues. At 535nm, a deep green, another set of cones gives its most enthusiastic response. At 575nm, a strong red, the third set has its peak response, tailing off into oranges. This is our trichromatic visual system.

The colour you perceive is calculated by combining the signals from these three types of cone. Pure red, green and blue light will each produce a peak response from one of those cone types, and nothing from the other two. What about other colours? Here, it's the combination of responses that determines perception. Crucially, the cones have overlapping responses. Yellow light, for example, will produce a partial response from the green cones and also a partial response from the red cones. When your brain receives partial activation from the green cones, plus partial activation from the red cones, it computes that you are perceiving yellow light.

This trichromatic system has an interesting quirk. Pure yellow light (around 580nm) will partially activate green and red cones, leading to the perception of yellow. However, there's another way to get exactly the same activation in the red and green cones: a partial green light shone at the same time as partial red light. This is why a red spotlight and a green spotlight overlapping will produce a yellow patch. It's why TV screens can show you every degree of colour by shining different combinations of tiny red, green and blue lights. The strange thing is that your brain has an identical response (seeing yellow) to two different physical phenomena: pure yellow light on the one hand, and a mixture of green and red light on the other.

I am emphasising this point because I had always thought, since seeing the demonstration in school, that when red and green lights are mixed, the wavelengths of light change and average out to become a single yellow wavelength. That is not the case at all. Due to our trichromatic system, two things that are physically different in the world look identical to us. However, this doesn't apply to everyone.

Mutant interior decorators

As already noted, our visual system is tuned to give a maximum response to three particular wavelengths. Other creatures with trichromatic vision, such as bees, are tuned to three different wavelengths of light. This means that particular patterns of light that look identical to us (such as yellow and red-green) look like different colours to bees, and we can see colours they can't. In fact, you can photograph a flower bed with a special camera and then alter how it processes light to simulate what a bee sees. Many flowers that look solid yellow to us have patterns and blobs of colour that bees can distinguish. The flowers around us have designs we can't see, because they did not evolve to please us.

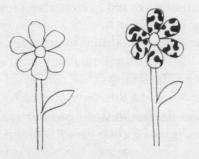

Meanwhile, some humans do not have trichromatic vision. They have cones that respond maximally to only two different wavelengths of light. They are colour-blind. Just as trichromatic people cannot tell the difference between red-green light and yellow, to some colour-blind people a yellow-green colour looks identical to yellow-reds, because they are missing the set of cones that would allow them to distinguish those colours.

Before lording this fact over your colour-blind friends, consider that to most of the animal kingdom us trichromats are also colour-blind. Most birds have four sets of cones, so they are tetrachromats. They can distinguish and probably experience colours that humans cannot. To birds, that red-green mix would look different to yellow light, and it is almost impossible for us to imagine what that would be like. Can you picture a colour you have never experienced before?

What would it be like to be a tetrachromat? It was discovered only quite recently that, remarkably, there are human mutants – almost always female, and typically painters or interior decorators – who are tetrachromatic. Of course, to say that they are mutants is pejorative. We are all the product of mutation. I mean mutants in the *X-Men* sense that they can do something really cool that the rest of us cannot.

The genes that grow photoreceptors are on the X chromosome. Women have two of these, whereas men only have one, which is why men are much more likely to be colour-blind. Normally, we have two copies of each gene; one is dominant, the other is recessive. In some women, both of their genes become active when their photoreceptors are growing, so as a result of this competition between genes, four different cone types are grown.

Such people are very rare indeed, but you might be one of them. The few that have been discovered do tend to be people who work with colour in some way. It's very curious that it has taken science so long to discover people who can see colours that others cannot, but we'll return to that point later. Rather than stop our discussion of colour perception with tetrachromats, I want to introduce you to one of my favourite animals: the mantis shrimp.

Quick off the mark

The mantis shrimp is a little fellow, about the size of your thumb, coloured in the most flamboyant display of swirls and dots. Although it's dressed like a Venetian duke ready for a carnival, the mantis shrimp has the soul of a drunk football hooligan – it just wants to fight. The mantis shrimp is a pugilistic little bastard that would break your similar-sized thumb if you put your hand in an aquarium to pet it. In fact, they have to be kept in bulletproof tanks because they can smash their way through regular glass. Pound for pound, they possess the biggest punch in the animal kingdom. If you had the same arm strength as a mantis shrimp scaled up to your size, you'd be able to throw a tennis ball into orbit and knock out a satellite. They are also mean, spending most of their time hiding among the rocks, getting into brawls with passers-by over territory.

While impressive, the mantis shrimp's fists are not as remarkable as its eyes. Most of us have three cone types; birds, reptiles and amphibians usually have four. Some insects and a couple of bird species have five types of cone cells. The mantis shrimp has more, and not just a few more: it has *sixteen* different cone types.

Not only are those cone types tuned to different wavelengths of light, some mantis shrimps even have cells that are tuned to different polarities of light (the orientation of light waves). Just like those glasses you get at a 3D movie that let in light at either a horizontal or vertical orientation, there are cells that selectively respond to polarity. For the mantis shrimp, it's not just vertical or horizontal polarity; they are even sensitive to light waves that are polarised in a spiral pattern.

These little creatures have a dizzying array of cone types. People are often astonished when they meet a colour-blind person for the first time. One such friend once told me with a sigh how many times people who find out his condition immediately raid their pencil case and demand that he tell them how he can't see the distinction between the colours. The difference between my friend and others is just the addition of one cone type. The mantis shrimp has thirteen additional cone types to us. What are the qualia of a mantis shrimp? What is the gulf in colour experience between us? What unimaginable kaleidoscope does it inhabit? Just how superpowered is its colour vision?

The surprising answer is that it sucks. Mantis shrimp are lousy at colour perception. Years after we understood the remarkable physiology of a mantis shrimp's eye, researchers tested its ability to discriminate colours in an experiment similar to the one we performed on our time-travelling Homer. They showed the shrimp a target patch of colour and trained it to choose one of two colour patches that matched it. When the shrimp got it right, it was rewarded with a snack.

Running this experiment many times, you can figure out how similar two colours can be before the shrimp is at even fifty per cent accuracy – in other words, when it is just guessing. You can do the same experiment with humans, too. The test gives two colours that are virtually the same to the shrimp, but are clearly different to our eyes. Although we have three cone types to their sixteen, we are way better at colour perception than mantis shrimps.

So why does the mantis shrimp have the most impressive arsenal of colour receptors, but no special ability to see colours? It seems to be like a toddler with a microscope: all that machinery but seemingly no interest or ability in using it. This is a speculative answer, but one with a crucial insight into what we mean by 'seeing' colour.

We have been discussing a creature that lives in a very specific ecosystem and has evolved with specific behavioural patterns. Matching colour patches to test perception has more in common with a DIY shop than a coral reef. This matters if we want to understand how the mantis shrimp sees colour. As a territorial creature, it fights other mantis shrimp, but some are better fighters than others. Before punching out at an intruder, a mantis shrimp has to recognise if the intruder is stronger or weaker and if it should fight or flee. On the one hand, this decision is easy in the sense that each mantis shrimp is distinctively and brightly patterned; on the other, it's very difficult as it has make that decision very quickly. Mantis shrimp have the fastest punch in the sea, so there's no time to dither.

Here's the hypothesis. In human vision, the output of the three cone types is integrated to produce the perception of a single colour, as described above. We can then use that perception – that yellow quale – to learn about yellow things: to choose a paint colour, figure out if the fruit is ripe, or just to enjoy the colour of the sunset. Maybe the shrimp doesn't need yellow qualia for all that. It just wants to decide if it needs to punch another mantis shrimp or not. That step of integrating the activation from three cones types into a single yellow quale takes time. Maybe the shrimp just skips that step. The hypothesis is that the raw output from its huge array of colour cone types gets fed immediately to the parts of its brain that command punching or fleeing. It needs that sensitivity to identify the lurid patterns of enemy combatants as quickly as possible. It doesn't need to integrate all those cone activations into a sensation of a single colour.

I remember once listening to an Olympic sprinter describe how he had shaved a few milliseconds off his 100-metres time by training himself to, as he described it, 'go on the "B" of the bang'. In other words, you or I might hear the bang of the starting gun, and once we had recognised that whole sound it would trigger a leap out of the blocks. By that time, our Olympic sprinter would be long gone.

Similarly, the mantis shrimp gains vital seconds of punching or fleeing time by responding immediately to colour signals. What it loses is the ability to integrate them into some sort of sensation that it can then use to complete weird tasks, such as matching colour patches for a scientist.

This seems like a good hypothesis to explain the behaviour, the neural processing and the evolution of the mantis shrimp and its remarkable colour vision. However, it doesn't really answer our central question of whether it sees the same blue as we do. Although we will never be able to see colour through the mantis shrimp's eyes, recent technological advances may soon give us the chance to experience new colours and a glimpse into its world.

Monkey see, monkey do

Monkeys mostly have two types of cone, like a colour-blind human. Scientists can show this behaviourally by asking a monkey to tap a red square on a touch screen to get a reward. Somewhat meanly, you can also place the red square against a background of blue blobs, which the poor colour-blind monkey can't see – it therefore just presses at random.

Recently, two researchers did an amazing thing. They took a virus and injected it into a monkey's eyeball. Viruses have many devious ways to break into cells and take over their DNA-replicating machinery, as they can't replicate alone. The researchers added a passenger to this virus, a small fragment of DNA that coded for a third type of cone cell. The virus did its job and broke into the eye cells, depositing the extra DNA. Over time, these genes took effect, and the colour-blind monkey grew a third type of cone cell for the first time in its species' history.

The researchers returned the monkey to the touch screen and watched expectantly. To begin with, it still pressed at random. Then, after some time and somewhat prosaically, the monkey simply tapped on the red square – the square that was previously invisible to it. From the outside, this is nothing remarkable, just a monkey tapping on a red square. However, what was happening inside the monkey's head? It could now discriminate a colour that only it, and none of its ancestors, was able to see. What did that new colour look like?

We may be able to find out. There is nothing in the procedure that was done with the monkey that could not be done, in theory, to a colour-blind human. Practically and ethically, there are still challenges with injecting a live virus into a human eyeball to alter a person's DNA. However, in theory, science could restore three-colour vision to a colour-blind person. What's more, we might be able to give tetrachromatic vision to a regular trichromatic person. That person, for the first time, would be able to see a colour that they, and perhaps no one else, will have ever seen.

#TheDress

Before we attempt such science-fiction experiments, there is still a problem we have to solve: that dress. Why is it that different people can look at the same picture and swear that it shows different colours? Perhaps surprisingly, we don't have a full answer yet, but there is some interesting speculation.

Your visual system is very good at ignoring what we call ambient light. The wavelength of light coming from objects is actually produced by two things. It's a function of the object itself and how it reflects light, and the colour of the light source illuminating it. Light sources change all the time. If you were to take a light meter and actually measure the wavelengths coming off your clothes, you'd get hugely different values as you moved inside to outside, in and out of shadows. Your brain is very good at ignoring these variations, otherwise you'd be continually shocked by your colour-changing clothes. You factor out these local variations in lighting in the process of interpreting the 'true' colour of things.

The peculiar thing about the image of the dress is that it appears to be lit by two different light sources. The dress is in a shop window; it gets some light from inside the shop and some from outside. The speculation is that some people are factoring out the ambient light from inside the shop, and others are factoring out the light from outside. These lights are slightly different colours, so depending on which you factor out, you perceive a differently coloured object.

Worldwide surveys have uncovered some patterns in the colours that people see in the dress. Women, older people and early risers tend to see gold and white; men, younger people and late risers, black and blue. In other words, perhaps some people have a preference for outdoor lighting because they get up early and see more daylight, but others who get out of bed later have more experience with indoor lighting. These lifelong experiences perhaps lead to a different light source being factored out of the image, so a white and gold – or a blue and black – dress appears.

Whether we see the same colour or not depends not just on the objective wavelength of light, but also on the context from which it emerges. Your brain does not perceive things in isolation, in absolute values. It guesses and interprets from context. We guess and interpret based on experience, and each of us can have slightly different experiences of the world. Even differences such as when you get out of bed in the morning change your lifetime experience of ambient light, so that one day, looking at a picture of a dress on the internet, you can perceive starkly different colours than the person sitting next to you.

Colour vs man

In trying to answer the simple question of whether we see the same blue, we have tried to find the path between *blue* (a wavelength of light in the world) and *blue* (an experience of a colour in the mind). We have found ourselves wandering through the physics of light, the biochemistry of our retina and the learning history of our brains. There is a third aspect to the question that we haven't even touched on yet. There is also *blue* (the word deriving from the Old French 'blo'). Is that concept the same for two people discussing the question, or between two cultures with different words for the hue of the sea?

We began with Gladstone, discussing Homer's wine-dark sea and his strange perception of colour. If he and other ancient Greeks were colour-blind, it seems they were not alone. Archeolinguists, as they call themselves, have trawled other ancient texts such as the Torah and the Old Testament in the Christian tradition, and found that there is no word blue used at all. If the ancient Greeks did have a genetic inability to see blue, it was shared with others. In the next chapter, we'll examine the first uses of the word blue in ancient texts and why it appeared when it did. We'll see that a deep understanding of the colour blue means that we have to think more broadly about the relationship between words, thoughts and things.

The blue we see is a result of physics, biochemistry and our personal experiences

Mind vs words

Are we defined by language?

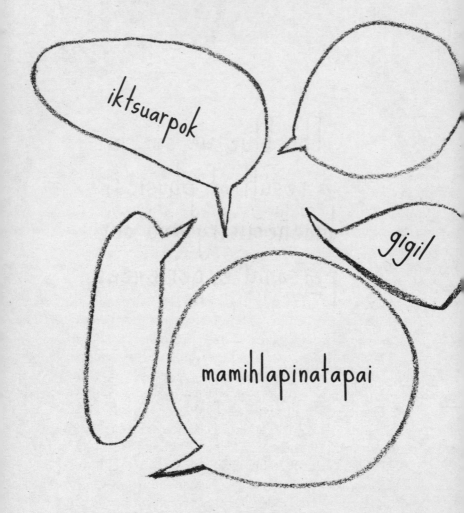

You are throwing a party and waiting for guests to arrive. You have one person who you're really hoping to see, but as you stand by the door, checking your watch for the third time, you realise that they're not coming. In that moment, you are experiencing the sadness of *iktsuarpok*. Then, your special person does appear! You lock eyes, sharing *mamihlapinatapai*, the wordless, yet meaningful look between two people who desire each other but are both reluctant to admit it. Your *kilig*, the butterflies you get whenever you're near someone attractive, give way to *gigil*, an irresistible urge to squeeze that person because you like them so much. Excitedly, you take them by the hand to introduce them to your friends, saying, 'I'd love you to meet…' – but your mind freezes and somehow you find you have forgotten their name. You have just *tartled* in front of them.

These words for feelings come from diverse cultures, from the Inuit *iktsuarpok* and Yaghan *mamihlapinatapai*, to the Tagalog *kilig* and *gigil* and Scots *tartle*. They might be new to you, but the feelings they describe may well be familiar. Even if you haven't experienced them, you could perhaps imagine them. Or perhaps you could not (I have only ever felt an irresistible urge to squeeze bubble wrap). How does having a word for something – an object, colour or sensation – change our ability to understand, imagine or experience it? In this chapter, we'll pick our way through one of the most contentious arguments in psychology: the relationship between words, thoughts and things.

Battle of the sexes

Let's begin with colour once again. We all experience colour, although the experiences can differ, as we've already seen. Across the world, people have different names for particular colours and different numbers of colour terms that they use to divide up the spectrum. Thinking again about blue, what parts of the colour spectrum correspond to that linguistic label, and are they the same for all people? The anthropologist Brent Berlin worked with linguist Paul Kay on some of the first scientific studies of this question in the 1960s and 1970s, taking a bag of colour chips to different parts of the world to discover how people described them.

More recently, cartoonist Randall Munroe, who draws a wonderful online comic strip called *xkcd*, came across another cartoon that showed a spectrum of twenty-nine colours. On the left of the chart, each colour was given a name, such as 'maraschino', 'eggplant', 'sea foam', and so on. The list was titled,

'Color names if you're a girl'. On the right of the chart, the colours were grouped into just seven names, such as 'red', 'orange' and 'blue'. That list was titled, 'Color names if you're a guy'. Women, according to this, see more colours. Munroe of course recognised this as the sort of battle-of-the-sexes joke that has sustained subpar stand-up comedians for years. However, he also recognised it as something much more interesting: a hypothesis.

Munroe realised he could collect the data to see if women and men really do use different numbers of colour terms. He showed visitors to his website a patch of colour from a random point in the colour spectrum and asked them to describe it in one word. Over 200,000 people responded. Munroe was then able to produce an empirically generated version of the cartoon, with the colour names that women *actually* used most commonly on the left, and the ones that men used most commonly on the right. He found that the words are more or less the same. There are a couple more types of green and pink on the left, but the sexes see and describe colours in essentially the same way. The joke is untrue.

Munroe also looked at the outlier responses; on the relatively rare occasions when the sexes differed, how did they differ? Colour terms used by women that were almost never used by men included 'dusty teal' and 'butter yellow' – names that looked as if they came from the cartoon. Then he looked for the responses given by men, but almost never by women. The top five were, 'penis', 'gay', 'WTF', 'dunno' and 'baige' (sic). What does this tell us? Men see colours the same way, but are way more likely to arse around in a survey than women. Also, they can't spell beige.

The language of LEGO

Colour perception between the sexes is the same, but what about colour perception between speakers of different languages? Homer did not seem to have a word for blue, but Russians have two words for the blue we know today. *Siniy* (синий) is a deeper, royal blue, while *goluboy* (голубой) is a lighter, sky blue. On the other hand, the Berinmo tribe of Papua New Guinea have only five colour names in total. They have words for dark and light, *kel* and *wap*, *mehi* for red, plus *wor* and *nol* that correspond roughly to a brownish green and a light blue. The Himba people of Namibia also have five colour terms, although they correspond to different colours.

Let's think more broadly about how language affects thought. You may have heard that Inuit languages have somewhere between 30 and 200 words for snow. Not living in the Arctic, we might open the curtains one morning and think, 'Damn it, snow! I'll be late for work.' An Inuit person might gaze out at a similar scene and possibly have richly different thoughts about whether this particular type of snow will settle or melt away, or how the texture will impact on being able to get around.

The hypothesis is that the language you speak determines how you see and think about the world. It is known as the 'linguistic relativity' hypothesis and was articulated most famously in 1940 by the linguist Benjamin Whorf: 'The world is presented in a kaleidoscopic flux of impressions which has to be organised by our minds – and this means largely by the linguistic systems in our minds.'

We think in words, therefore we can only think of things for which we have words. That's the strongest possible version of the idea of linguistic relativity, but it is probably too strong. At the start of this chapter, I was able to explain in English words what *gigil* and *iktsuarpok* mean by assuming a common experience. Since we can learn new words from other languages, and even create new words, we cannot be entirely imprisoned by any given language.

A more plausible version of the linguistic relativity hypothesis is that language does not strictly confine thought, but influences, determines or shapes it. An Inuit translator could patiently explain things to you, circumlocuting in many English words what is meant by one Inuit word; Inuit people themselves are more attuned to types of snow or disappointment in friends because of the presence of those words in their language.

The relationship between words and thoughts has been explored by poets and philosophers with metaphors and metaphysics. As a prosaic psychologist, I think more in terms of LEGO sets from my childhood.

If what you can understand is what you can build in LEGO, then the words in our language are the different bricks that you possess. They limit what you can build, but it's a soft constraint. Even with only rectangular

Do language 'kits' always fit together?

bricks you can still approximate a round tower with a bit of ingenuity. You might get lucky one Christmas and be given a medieval castle LEGO set, which comes with curved wall sections. Now you can build more efficiently and effectively. This is like learning a new word.

The question of linguistic relativity, how whole language systems shape thought, is like taking your box of LEGO to meet the kids who just moved in next door. Will their LEGO bricks be similar enough that you can build together? Will they just have different lengths and colours of blocks that eventually fit together, or will they have LEGO Technic, with hinges, cogs and gears – all things your LEGO could never hope to emulate? Or worse, will they have some new type with triangular blocks that never interlock?

Linguistic relativity provides one of the great arm wrestles of academic psychology. Are the differences in the words we have relatively small and arbitrary, so that we can talk our way around them and build a common understanding? Or are the differences so fundamental that there are things you can say (and things you can think) in one language that you just cannot in another?

What if it snowed?

In the 1980s, the linguist and psychologist Alfred Bloom wanted to discover if people from China could use counterfactual reasoning. Counterfactuals are 'what if?' statements, which we use all the time in English. What if the Germans had won the Second World War? What if

Ross and Phoebe got together in *Friends*? There doesn't seem to be an equivalent in Chinese languages.

Bloom visited men in the countryside and asked questions such as, 'If you had been born a girl, what would your life be like?'. Invariably, the men would look confused, then reply that they were male. He asked them about what life might be like if they had been born in Japan, but the men generally responded that they were actually born in China. It seemed to Bloom that it was very hard for them to comprehend counterfactual ideas.

Consider the wider patterns of history. Fifteenth-century China was a remarkable place, with a stable government, a civil service, sophisticated arts and science, irrigation and fireworks. Meanwhile, Europe was a backwards mudhole of small regional monarchies locked in endless wars. That period is called the Dark Ages for good reason. However, from the Renaissance onwards, Europe began a series of revolts in religion, government, art and science that shaped the modern world; China stayed pretty much the same.

Why were the fates of these two peoples so different over the past 500 years? Perhaps it was because of their languages. Europeans, able to easily pose counterfactuals, could continually think about what could happen if they didn't have to follow a certain king or church, or if they could discover knowledge by experimentation. While they began in cultural squalor, they could dream of better things. The Chinese were stuck in their patterns of life, blinkered by the structure of their languages to the possibility of something better.

This was the promise of the linguistic relativity hypothesis: that swathes of history and culture could be related to patterns of language and thought. However, there is a problem with this conclusion, in particular with the cases of Inuit snow and Chinese counterfactuals. The facts presented are, in the words of linguist Geoffrey Pullum, 'unredeemed piffle'.

The fact that Inuit people have many words for snow can be seen in textbooks, newspaper articles and endless 'fascinating facts' compilations on cereal boxes and magazines. However, it is simply not true – it has never really been true at all. It is piffle that, for some reason, has been repeated, exaggerated and asserted so often that it has taken on the appearance of truth. Or at least, no one bothered to check to see if it was true, or to listen to anthropologists such as Laura Martin, who had been saying all along that it was nonsense.

It seems that Inuit languages really have only two words for snow: *qanik*, for when snow is in the air, and *aput*, for when it is on the ground. Like English, they have words to modify those, such as hard, cold and icy. As linguists such as Steven Pinker have pointed out, English has many words for snow: sleet, slush, blizzard, avalanche, hail, hardpack, powder, flurry, dusting, and so on. Even if Inuit languages did have many words for snow (which they don't), they would not be unusual.

What about the Chinese and their counterfactually limited thought? Rewind to the moment Bloom spoke to the people he interviewed. Reviewing his notes, it turns out that what he was actually asking them was something akin to, 'Girl born are you what now?'. No wonder those men looked at him blankly. It's not that they couldn't conceive of counterfactuals, it's just that Bloom was speaking their language really badly.

The idea that Europe was a place of innovation, while China was a place of rigid stagnation, was appealing to some writers at the time, so rather than stopping to check Bloom's data, they ran with the idea of language shaping the destiny of nations. Of course, that historical narrative is highly dubious. China had many periods of revolution in its history, while Europe had many periods of stagnation. As Martin said about the beliefs people have about the Inuit peoples, 'we are prepared to believe almost anything' about groups that are unfamiliar or foreign to us.

Nut-eating elephants

Since the mid-1990s, the strong version of linguistic relativity seemed debunked among psychologists. The majority opinion seems to be that we have our thoughts and we can translate them into any given language. Words are a tool, and while some languages might have better tools for certain jobs, human thought is flexible and powerful enough that it is not limited or constrained by any individual language. However, recent experiments are suggesting that linguistic relativity is not quite dead as an idea, it has just retreated. Colour is one of the areas in which it is making a small comeback.

Consider the sentence, 'the elephant ate the nuts'. When did the eating take place? As an English speaker, you can tell me that it was in the past, because the verb 'to eat' has been modified into the past tense 'ate'. If you said that sentence in Indonesian and asked when it happened, the person answering would have no reply. In Indonesian, you do not have to specify time by modifying the verb. One could choose to add words and say, 'the elephant ate the nuts last week', but it's not mandatory to build that information into the verb itself. Similarly, I could ask, 'What genitals did the elephant have?'. As an English speaker, you would have no idea and perhaps be a little creeped out by the question. If I had asked the same question in Russian, the person would be able to answer. In Russian, you have to specify the sex of the elephant to ask the question.

Finally, I could enquire, 'Did you see the elephant eat these nuts – did you speak to someone who saw this first-hand – or is this just some sort of nut-eating rumour you heard?'. We simply don't know from the

English question. If it was asked in Turkish, then the person would have had to state if they had first-hand knowledge, second-hand, or heard a rumour. Just as we have to modify the verb according to time, Turkish modifies it according to the level of certainty.

In this case, English, Russian and Turkish speakers could all understand each other and all of these facts about the elephant and the nuts. They are not imprisoned by their language, unable to imagine seeing a male elephant eating nuts in the future. However, the subtler version of the linguistic relativity hypothesis asks if their thoughts are influenced by the demands of their language. Would Turkish speakers make better journalists and judges because their language demands that they pay attention to certainty in every sentence?

Cognitive scientist Lera Boroditsky performed an ingenious set of experiments with Indonesian speakers to test such perceptions. They do not modify verbs according to the time that an event took place. They have clocks and calendars like the rest of us, but time is not built into Indonesian verb structure as it is in English. She took pictures of people about to kick a football, at the moment of kicking a football, and having just kicked a football. There were several different people in these three poses, mixed up in a stack of pictures. Boroditsky then asked English speakers to sort them into piles of pictures that were similar to each other. The instructions didn't mention time, football, or anything other than the idea that similar things should go together. In other words, she was trying to find out what similarity meant to the participants.

English speakers tended to put all the people who were about to kick the ball in one pile, all the people

kicking the ball in another, and all the people who had just kicked the ball in a third pile. They used time to organise their thoughts. But perhaps that is just the natural way anyone would sort the images.

When Boroditsky travelled to Indonesia to perform the same experiment, however, Indonesian speakers tended to put all the pictures of one person in one pile, all the pictures of a different person in another, and so on. Time was not how they organised the pictures to judge similarity. To them, similar pictures were of the same person. They could see that different things were happening, but it seemed less relevant.

One might object that this is perhaps a cultural difference. Maybe individual identity is more important in Indonesia. The same experiment was run with people who were bilingual in English and Indonesian. If the instructions to sort the pictures were given in Indonesian, the participants sorted mostly by person; when instructed in English, sorted by time. Finally, Boroditsky directed English speakers to perform the same task, but asked them to recite numbers in their head. The hypothesis was that reciting numbers would, in a sense, tie up verbal processing and reduce the influence of language upon the task. Accordingly, while uttering numbers, English speakers tended to sort the pictures by person, more like the Indonesian participants.

Russian blues

Now we can go back to colour. Although people across the world can, broadly speaking, see colours equally well, how might the fact that they have five, seven, ten or twenty colour terms change how they think about colour? Boroditsky carried out experiments with Russian and English speakers, and a lot of blue blobs.

Her task was simple. One blob of colour was shown at the top of a screen, and two at the bottom. Participants had to press a button to indicate which of the two blobs at the bottom matched the target at the top. There were many trials, with many different colours, but Boroditsky was interested in two types of trial in particular. In one, the two blobs at the bottom were both the type of blue Russian speakers would call *siniy*, the deeper, royal blue. One of them was around ten per cent lighter than the other, but they were both *siniy*, and only one matched the *siniy* blob at the top. In the second type of trial, there were still two blue blobs differing by about ten per cent, but one was now called *goluboy*. That ten per cent difference happened to straddle the boundary between the two colours.

If you gave this task to a robot with a light meter, the two trials would be equally difficult. In both, you have to discriminate blues ten per cent apart and match one of them to the target. To an English-speaking human the trials are also equally difficult: they are all just types of blue. However, the Russian speakers were faster at the second trial, when the two blobs were *siniy* and *goluboy*, rather than *siniy* and a slightly lighter *siniy*. In other words, the presence of a linguistic label gave them a processing boost. And yet, just like the English speakers sorting football pictures, when the Russian speakers recited numbers in their head, the processing boost went away. Thinking of numbers was enough to engage and occupy the language-processing part of the brain so it couldn't contribute to the colour task, and the

Russian speakers matched colour blobs more like the English speakers.

Back to Homer

What about Homer? The evidence we saw in the last chapter was that he didn't have a word for blue in his language. Subjecting him to psychology experiments, we can speculate that he would have given the same name to blue chips as reds or greens, just like some cultures today. If we asked if two chips were identical or not, he would have been able to see the difference as easily as we could. He probably had the same mechanisms of colour perception and would make the same discriminations as we would. If we timed his responses carefully, we would find that as you or I would be quicker to discriminate blue chips from green chips than two types of (equally different) blue, Homer would not show this difference. Just like the English speakers insensitive to *siniy* and *goluboy*, he wouldn't get a processing boost from a label for 'blue'.

If we allowed Homer to take a look at our world after the experiments, I'm sure there would be many sights that would stagger him. There might be one thing particularly shocking to him, though, if only he were able to find the words to express it: the sheer number of blue things.

The problem is, even if we have correctly described Homer's colour behaviour in the lab, we are still missing the answer to a really big question. Why is it that he didn't have a word for blue in the first place? The nineteenth-century linguist Lazarus Geiger put forward a very interesting hypothesis about this.

Geiger tracked the emergence of colour terms across history and many different languages and found an intriguing pattern. The first colour terms in the history of a language are always black and white, or some form of light and dark. Red comes next, then you'll find mention of yellow and green. Blue is always last. Always. More remarkably, the moment when blue did appear in ancient Greek coincides with another historical event: the opening of trade routes to the east. More specifically, blue emerges with the period that a particular type of stone, mined in what is now Afghanistan, entered the Greek world: the bright blue lapis lazuli.

Here's the extraordinary claim: until lapis lazuli entered the Greek world, there weren't really many blue things there. Before you snort in disbelief, consider that there are very few blue animals. Perhaps a blue jay bird, or some exotic fish, but there are no blue mammals. There are no blue plants or foods (nowadays blue flowers have generally been bred artificially). Blue dye and paint was extremely rare for a long time, as it is chemically very hard to produce, and was precious once it was created. Ultramarine, the blue paint produced from lapis lazuli, was revered in Europe when it was eventually imported in the Middle Ages. It was reserved for figures such as the Virgin Mary; the blue headscarf outshines the pearl earring worn by the girl in Vermeer's famous painting.

In Homer's time, before lapis lazuli, there weren't many blue things, so he didn't need the word. Homer would never say, 'I think I'll wear a blue toga today', or 'He lives in the blue house', any more than he'd say 'What's the wifi password?' or 'Do you have that in gluten-free?'. Those things just weren't part of his world, so there was no need to name them. The ancient Greeks did not have a word for blue.

If you have ever been on holiday in Greece you might be screaming in objection to this argument. How can we say the ancient Greeks had no blue when they would have had beautiful blue skies and seas? That's true, of course, but the counter argument is that while they are undoubtedly blue things, they are relatively constant and unchanging. You don't need to name and discriminate the colour of the sky or sea. It's like a constant background noise you stop hearing, so would never need to name.

We tend to think of words as being labels for things. In the case of colour, we talk about it as if words are labels for our qualia, such as the internal sensations we have looking at the blue sky. But how can we *really know* that we experience the same blue? The response at which we've arrived is that perhaps words are not labels for internal experiences; they are tools to discriminate between objects in the world. If that world does not contain many objects that need to be discriminated in that way, there will not be a word for them. It would be a tool without a use. Blue, for Homer, was a screwdriver before there were screws.

Words vs man

It's not that language imprisons thought and constrains us to one way of thinking about the world. It's not that language blinds us to the world and only allows us to see what we can name. Rather, the language we speak is able to bias, influence and nudge how we think. It will highlight one way of being similar over another, draw attention to the difference between two colour patches and gloss over the difference between another. It will allow a feeling to be named and articulated, rather than just felt. On the one hand, these differences between the speakers of different languages seem widespread and profound; on the other, they can be so shallow that they disappear when someone simply ties up the language processing in their brain by reciting numbers. If you feel both *gigil* and *kilig* when you meet someone from another linguistic culture, but are worried that you can't bridge the divide, don't *mamihlapinatapai,* just ask for their phone number.

Mind vs man

Are we all racist?

There were many astonishing moments during the 2016 US presidential election. Two in particular have stuck in my mind, both from the debates between Donald Trump and Hillary Clinton. In one, Trump said, 'Nobody has more respect for women than I do. Nobody.' Some in the audience burst into laughter. They were perhaps thinking at that moment of the dozen or so women who were accusing Trump of sexual assault, the remarks he made on tape boasting of 'grabbing' women, or maybe the simple fact that he owned the Miss Universe franchise for many years, the defining purpose of which is to objectify women and judge them on their appearance. Yet in Trump's mind, nobody respected women more. The moderator of the debate had to ask the audience to keep quiet. A few weeks later, Trump won the presidency, and one of his first acts was to sign an order restricting access to information about birth control from American organisations for women in developing countries. Nobody was laughing then.

The other moment that had struck me occurred a few weeks earlier. The backdrop to the debate was the

Black Lives Matter movement, which was mobilising across the country in protests about the number of black Americans who were being killed by police. The moderator asked Clinton if she believed that the police were 'implicitly biased against black people'. Clinton replied that she thought 'implicit bias is a problem for everyone, not just police'. The audience was silent, but the remark produced a howl of outrage online. Being racist is universally seen as a Bad Thing, and Clinton had just said that all Americans are racist. In a spectacular contortion of victimhood, some in the right-wing media reported that Clinton had said that all *white people* were racist, and then condemned her for being racist herself against white people.

These two statements revealed a gulf in political attitudes towards sex and race. However, what fascinated the nerdy psychologist in me was the gulf in understanding of what prejudice and attitudes really are.

Let's assume that Trump spoke sincerely: in his mind, he believes he respects women, so how could anyone

think he was biased against them? Perhaps to him, the Miss Universe pageants were a mark of that respect. He just wanted to give awards to the best women because he respects them so much. To his supporters, Trump's remarks and treatment of women weren't evidence of an attitude that was troubling. Indeed, more white women voted for him than for Clinton.

In complete contrast, Clinton endorsed the view that prejudice and bias are part of how all our minds work. To counteract their potential effect on behaviour requires vigilance and training, especially for people such as police officers, whose actions can have grave consequences. If this is true, then to some degree we are all racist.

Politics aside, which of these views is supported by scientific evidence? Are attitudes shown by what you say or what you do? What is this 'implicit bias' that supposedly lurks beneath the surface in our minds? Are all people really prejudiced against other groups, or is that just politically correct liberal guilt that has manifested itself

in a slur on the honour of white Americans? What about you, the reader of this book? You might be a world away from the racial politics of the US, but are you prejudiced against those of a different gender, or people from other countries, or those with different sexual orientations or religions to your own? Let's find out.

Measuring attitudes

To start, we need to define what an attitude is. Social psychologists have thought a lot about this. Attitudes – how to describe, measure and influence them – were one of the defining issues of social psychology as it developed in the shadow of the Second World War, trying to account for how such extremes of belief and action produced the Nazi movement. In the classic conceptual definition, an attitude was framed as a combination of affect, behaviour and cognition – the ABC of attitudes. An attitude must be related to affect: in the simplest case, it has to be a positive or negative emotional evaluation. It has to relate to behaviour in some way: to influence the things we vote for, listen to and buy. It has to be cognitive: we have to be able to know, think and express our own attitudes. Attitudes defined in this way were seen as the basic atoms of psychological science.

For an attitude to be a thing of science, of course, we also have to be able to measure it in some way. If you aren't counting things, you aren't doing science. Measuring attitude atoms seems to be pretty straightforward – we can just use a survey, like in a magazine. To measure attitudes towards black Americans, for example in 2002, psychologists David

Sears and PJ Henry put to people statements such as, 'Generations of slavery and discrimination have created conditions that make it difficult for Blacks [sic] to work their way out of the lower class', or 'Over the past few years, Blacks have gotten less than they deserve'. They gave people a scale on which to indicate how much they agreed, averaged those numbers, and produced a measure of people's racial attitudes.

Millions of such attitude surveys have been done in the past few decades, in social psychology, market research and political polling. We measure attitudes all the time and can quantify their cognitive and emotional content. What about their connection to behaviour?

In a field study in the 1930s, at a time of widespread anti-Asian prejudice in the United States, a social psychologist called Richard LaPiere surveyed racial attitudes towards people of Chinese origin. LaPiere measured these attitudes in a particular, practical way. He wrote to a selection of hotels, motels and dining establishments across the country, explaining that he was travelling with two Chinese guests and asking if it would be possible to reserve a room for the night (or a table). Of the 128 responses, ninety-one per cent of the hotels and ninety-two per cent of the diners and restaurants said they would refuse to serve them because they were Chinese. They were flat-out, openly racist answers. However, what all the respondents didn't know was that at least six months prior to receiving the questionnaire, LaPiere and the two Chinese guests had actually visited each establishment as customers. Remarkably, only one out of the 250 places they had originally planned to visit denied them service. So where did the racism go? What happened to attitudes as something that could explain and predict behaviour?

Making your mind up

Over the years, it has become increasingly obvious that LaPiere's study was not a fluke. Social psychologists have repeatedly measured people's attitudes to themes as diverse as cheating in school, going to church and using birth control. Those attitudes do not match up to measured behaviours – how much people cheat in exams, whether they go to church or if they use birth-control pills. Try this yourself: do you think eating five or more portions of fruit and vegetables a day is healthy? If you agree, do you actually eat five or more portions every single day?

If you find that there is dissociation between your attitude and behaviour, you're not alone. In meta-analyses of many such studies of attitudes versus behaviours, psychologists have found that the correlation between the two is astonishingly weak. In statistical terms, as little as two per cent of the variance in someone's behaviour is explained by their attitudes, a relationship strength that is typically interpreted as 'none' to 'weak'.

Why aren't attitudes doing their job? They are supposed to be cognitive things with affective value that predicts behaviour. Why aren't these atoms of social psychology behaving as they should? (Before you accuse psychologists of physics envy about understanding basic phenomena, physicists can't explain ninety-five per cent of the energy and matter in the universe.)

The first problem is that people lie. In social science, this is diplomatically known as 'self-presentation bias'. People don't tend to introduce themselves on a social media profile as, 'Keen golfer and avid homophobe' or 'Loves: yoga & cats, Hates: disabled people'. There are many attitudes that are seen as socially undesirable, and for good reason. Even people who rail against 'political correctness' will usually agree that prejudice is a bad thing. They might disagree with others about what counts as prejudice, but they are very unlikely to introduce themselves with a firm handshake and say, 'I'm a big racist, pleased to meet you!'

Self-presentation bias can influence the results of attitude surveys in many subtle ways, making them inaccurate measures of the supposedly true attitudes lying beneath. People will shift their answers according to who is asking the question and what they think the questioner wants to hear. In one case, researchers sent out surveys with little crime stories, in each case asking people to judge if the individual who had committed the crime was to blame, or the society they lived in. The survey came with a cover letter thanking people for participating, but it differed between recipients in one tiny way. The letterhead stated that the survey came from the 'Institute of Social Research' or the 'Institute of Personality Research', depending on who received it. If the survey came from the former, they were more likely to blame social variables; if it came from the latter, then the blame fell on personality variables. We tweak our answers to please the questioner.

Another problem with measuring attitudes is how you ask your questions. Even innocuous changes in wording can have a dramatic effect on answers. In one survey, when questioned if they got headaches *frequently*, and if so, how often, people answered about every three days. If they were asked if they got headaches *occasionally*, and if so, how often, they answered about every ten days. That former rate is more than three times higher in response to a tiny difference in phrasing. You might even have had to look back at the first question to notice what the difference was.

These problems exist when there are small changes to wording talking about objective things such as headaches. The problems are compounded when we are asking about more complex ideas and social attitudes. Only twenty-two per cent of people in an American survey said they were in favour of spending on welfare. The researchers asked the same people if they approved of giving financial support to people in poverty, to people made unemployed through no fault of their own, to disabled people, and so on. Across these government spending programmes, sixty-one per cent were in favour of 'assisting the poor', but these programmes are precisely what welfare is. Those questions were asking the same thing, but the response was different by a factor of almost three. We still don't know if people support welfare programmes by twenty-two or sixty-one per cent, either.

A secret agenda

Across the Atlantic, the future of the EU is a major topic of debate. Interactions between European states are massively complex, encompassing trade deals, immigration, human rights legislation and, of course, the Eurovision song contest. However, when all of the big issues involved are reduced to a single question – 'Should we be in Europe?' – people can interpret 'Europe' in vastly different ways.

If you wanted to understand someone's attitude to Europe, perhaps so you could persuade them to vote one way or another in a referendum, what would you do? One approach would be to drill down into someone's understanding, to endlessly survey their opinions and attitudes to different aspects of European integration. Then you can engage in a rational debate on those issues.

In chapter three, we saw that there are many ways in which people's behaviour, attitudes and decisions can be swayed by the forces of persuasion, cognitive dissonance and the dark arts of manipulation, either accidentally or with the deliberate purpose of biasing an answer. Consider answering these questions: 'Do you worry about uncontrolled immigration to this country?', 'Do you think British laws should be decided by British people?' and 'Do you think the UK should stay in the EU?'. Now consider these alternative questions: 'Do you think that being able to work and travel freely throughout the EU is a good thing?', 'Do you think that free trade with the EU helps the UK?' and 'Do you think the UK should stay in the EU?'. The evidence is that you'll get different answers to the last question because of people's need to appear consistent. However, if you only publish the results of that last question, then you have a handy way to argue whatever you wish about what the British people 'really think' about the EU.

There is another way. Everything we say publicly (perhaps to researchers) is known as our 'explicit attitudes'. However there are also 'implicit attitudes' – the associations, stereotypes and feelings we have about people, countries and ideas that we might not say out loud (and might not even be aware of), but nevertheless have an influence over our behaviour.

The tension between explicit and implicit attitudes was exploited by Karl Rove, senior advisor to former president George W Bush, in the run-up to the 2000 presidential election. In some American states, there are laws that place restraints on forms of aggressive political advertising, such as phoning people up at home. There are fewer restraints on polling; you can ask someone their explicit attitude towards something, as that doesn't count as overt persuasion. Only it does, of course, because asking someone their explicit opinion can activate implicit attitudes. It's called 'push polling'.

When Bush was fighting to become the Republican candidate against John McCain, Rove got his teams to ask people how they would feel if it transpired that a candidate for office had had a child out of wedlock. Sent along with the question was an image of McCain with a dark-skinned child. The aim was to associate McCain in the voters' minds with their negative attitudes to both adultery and non-white people. The child in the picture was indeed McCain's daughter. She was an orphan from Bangladesh who had been brought to the US by McCain's wife Cindy for medical treatment, and the couple had adopted her. Remarkably, Rove used the McCains' humanitarian act to stir negative racial attitudes against him.

In many recent political campaigns in Europe, similar tactics have been engaged. Rather than measuring or engaging with the rational processes behind people's explicit attitudes, advertisements and imagery are used to tap into fears of outsiders.

Canadians, lesbians and Texans

This is the idea that Hillary Clinton was putting forward – that people, regardless of what they might say explicitly, have implicit biases that determine their behaviour. What is the evidence that such implicit biases are real? Do they have an influence on behaviour? Or is this all a myth propagated by liberals?

It's easy to show that we all have a vast knowledge of associations between social groups and characteristics. For this experiment, put aside all your fears about political correctness and think of adjectives to describe the stereotypes of Canadians, lesbians and Texans.

My bet is that you and I (and anyone else from a comparable society) would have similar lists of adjectives. That's not to say any of those words would accurately describe those people. We may not have even met people from any of those groups, or we may have met lots and found them to be diverse people who defy generalisation. That said, we still know the stereotypes; they are part of the knowledge of our culture. If someone declares, 'I don't have stereotypes for people, I think of everyone as individuals', they are lying or naive. Rightly or wrongly, stereotypes are concepts that help us to structure our knowledge of the world.

Stereotypes are in all of our heads and influence our thinking, regardless of how we feel about that, and we have the scientific tools to prove it. No matter how unbiased and politically correct you think you are, I can demonstrate that you have racist, sexist and homophobic beliefs in your mind.

Before reading further, visit www.tinyurl.com/manvsmindiat and follow the links to take an Implicit Associations Test (IAT). You'll find different IATs based on various themes. These simple tests were developed in the 1990s by social psychologists, borrowing ideas from cognitive psychologists who had been studying how the brain processes and stores information.

In an IAT you are given a series of very simple categorisation tasks. For a test on racial associations, you have to press one key to categorise a picture of a face as white, and another key to categorise it as black, as a practice session. Then you categorise words, pressing a key if they are positive ('happy', 'laugh') and another key if they are negative ('angry', 'sickening'). After practising with the words, you are asked to categorise both pictures and words as they flash up in a random order. Finally, you repeat the task, but with a switch. Positive words are now categorised with the key you pressed for negative words and vice versa.

Regardless of your own personal ethnicity, if you are like the millions of other people in Europe and the US who have taken the test, I can predict what your data will look like. You will complete the task with little or no errors, as there is nothing difficult here. The information is in the speed of your responses. You'll be faster to press the buttons when you are categorising good words and white faces with one key, and bad words and black faces with the other. You'll be slower, by something like 100 milliseconds, when you have to press the same key to categorise black faces and good words, and white faces and bad words. The reason for this difference – the only reason – is that your brain finds it hard to group together the concepts of black faces and good things. There is interference. To your brain, those concepts are in conflict and you are slower to process them. Your brain is racist.

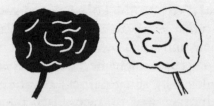

Unsurprisingly, you probably have many objections to this charge of racism. You might validly object that, in this example, you learned to pair white faces and good words together first, so maybe it's just hard to switch to black faces and good words. It is certainly true that we tend to be slowed down by a switch in tasks like this, but you can rerun the experiment to have black faces/good words and white faces/bad words appear first, then switch to white faces/good words and black faces/bad words. Over many experiments, despite changing both the pairing of concepts and the order in which they're learned, people are always slower when they are categorising black faces and good words, and white faces and bad words.

You might object that there's really only a tiny difference in reaction times. How can just 100 milliseconds make you racist? The size of the effect isn't the point. In physics, vast particle accelerators find tiny fluctuations in energy fields. It's not that those fluctuations matter themselves, as they are absolutely tiny. The point is that the only explanation for their particular existence at all is the presence of strange subatomic matter. Similarly, the point is not that the 100ms delay has any direct consequences; the only explanation for its existence at all is the presence of implicit prejudice in your brain. The experiment didn't put it there, it simply presents you with stimuli to categorise. The significance of the 100ms is that it tells us the knowledge in your brain is structured so that it apparently associates black people with bad things and white people with good things.

A final objection might be that this experiment is perhaps muddied by some particular feature of black and white. Independent of race, black things have a negative connotation, perhaps though association with darkness. A black heart, for example, is perceived to be evil. Maybe this explains the negative association? In response, this is where the power of the IAT lies. The same tool and experimental logic can be employed to look at associations between any two dimensions, not just race and positive-negative balance. As mentioned above, there are various IATs about different themes. By asking people to categorise two different types of stimuli, they can show that people tend to associate black faces with weapons, white faces with kitchen tools, female names with images of home life, and male names with the workplace, among many other examples.

There is also an IAT in which people characterise first names as male and female, and university subjects as humanities or science. What we see is that people reliably find it easier to associate males with science and females with humanities. I persuaded my wife to take part in this experiment and she showed the same bias, even though she is a scientist and her father was a professor of the humanities. This raises another key point about the biases revealed by the IAT: it doesn't matter if you yourself are a member of one social group or another. What the IAT is revealing is not your personal values, but the stereotypes and associations of the society you live in. Even if you are a black American, you will typically show the same negative association to images of black faces as the rest of American society; if you are a female scientist, you'll still implicitly associate science disciplines with male names.

Life-or-death judgements

By no means have we settled the question about whether we are all racist. You could take the IAT, see your key pressing is slower when pairing certain races with good words, but you could reply that it has nothing to do with attitudes, beliefs or values. After all, an IAT just tells you to stab at keys on a computer, not how you treat work colleagues, vote or choose who to sit next to on the train. Your implicit attitudes, or whatever it is that is influencing reaction times on the IAT, are quite probably different to your explicit attitudes. If we want to know your explicit attitudes, why don't we just ask for them?

That is exactly what one group of researchers did. They asked for people's opinions and still found that implicit attitudes were at work. In one experiment, carried out by my PhD supervisor Michael Spivey and colleagues, participants were asked directly about their explicit attitudes. They were given two options, 'like' and 'dislike', to click in response to words they heard in their headphones.

Stereotypes

Implicit
Attitudes

Explicit Attitudes

The participants, all white males, clicked away, giving their preferences for 'cakes', 'pain', 'smiles', and so on. When they heard 'black people', everyone clicked 'like'. After all, they weren't racist. However, the researchers didn't just look at which button the participants clicked. They tracked the precise trajectory of the mouse pointer from its starting position all the way to the 'like' option. For 'black people', but no other choices, there was a systematic deviation towards the 'dislike' option. Their explicit attitudes fired off a positive response, but their implicit prejudice was dragging the mouse pointer off course.

One might object that this is still a tiny behavioural blip. A few pixels of deviation in a mouse pointer, a few milliseconds slower on a click: these actions have no consequences in the world. They are not evidence of prejudice and are certainly not evidence for Hillary Clinton's suggestion that we are all racist.

Even small actions can have large consequences, though. Perhaps implicit prejudice does simply delay or speed-up actions for a few milliseconds. However, some people have only milliseconds to make life-or-death judgements. An armed police officer has to decide if a suspect is reaching for a gun or for identification. Indeed, scientists put officers in a virtual reality simulator where they had to quickly distinguish armed suspects from innocent bystanders. With black suspects – and sometimes bystanders – the officer's trigger finger twitched faster if they had stronger negative implicit attitudes.

Nurses who work in emergency departments have to make rapid triage decisions. When paramedics burst through the door, they have to decide which patients need to see a doctor immediately and who can afford to wait. In one study, when white nurses ranked black patients versus white on the triage list, the outcomes were predicted by their results on an IAT test.

Cultural toxicity

Even if we don't work under such pressure, we can be affected by implicit prejudice. Do you pause to hold open the door for the person behind you? It's a millisecond choice that might be predicted by measures of your implicit prejudice to the other person. It's a momentary action for you, but for the person who spends their day with many more doors swinging shut in their face, it has a different consequence. These acts of 'microaggression', tiny behaviours that are very different from explicit acts of racism, accrue an effect of their own over time. They might explain a paradox in American race relations. Most white people think their society is getting less racist towards black people, whereas black people see little or no change. One explanation is that white people see more black people in positions of wealth and authority around them – there was even a black president. For black people themselves, experience of racism has less to do with these very visible individuals and more to do with daily experiences of microaggression and prejudice.

Nevertheless, some people boldly claim to be 'colour-blind' when it comes to people, insisting they don't even notice race – with the implication that their judgements cannot be prejudiced. Once again, we can dismiss this with scientific evidence. If people recall anything at all about a person, they can remember their sex and something about their race. It just never happens that you can recall a person but not remember their race.

When people truly are blind to race or sex – in other words, they can't actually see the other person – their judgements measurably change. If musicians audition from behind a curtain, women are chosen more often. Whereas if a scientific paper has a female name at the top, it is less likely to get published. People are not blind to social categories and they are not immune to prejudice.

Implicit prejudice is present in most of us – regardless of who we are and how it applies to us – because we all grew up in the same culture, watching the same TV shows, seeing the same adverts. This is where all these associations come from: the world around us.

'Political correctness gone mad' is the response of some when people complain about the representation of minorities or women in the media. How can one slightly sexist TV character or a single Islamophobic comment harm anyone? It's true that each individual incidence of a sexist trope or ethnic stereotype won't cause irreparable damage, just like a single chocolate bar won't affect your health. Of course, if we live on a diet of such things – constant depictions of women as weak and helpless, men as leaders and achievers, black people as aggressors, Muslims as a threat – then the net result is a toxic mindset. It's no surprise that a leader such as President Trump can talk about women as he does or place restrictions on Muslims entering the country and a sizeable portion of Americans do not object.

Man vs man

All politics aside, Hillary Clinton was right. Ignore for the moment any questions of policies about equal pay, treatment of minorities, immigration, or same-sex marriage. Right-wing or left-wing, we all carry the implicit prejudices of the culture around us. The question is simply what we should do about it. Of course, one can never truly put aside all politics. Even though prejudice can be studied scientifically and demonstrated with experiments, it has become a divisive issue. Somewhat ironically, it is our attitudes towards attitude research that determine what we believe.

Implicit prejudice is not something that will go away when ignored; it is not banished by confident bluster about equality, or empty assertions that 'nobody has more respect for women than I do'. In fact, it's likely that the issue is going to dominate legal and political debates in the coming years.

It used to be the case that prejudice was only what you said. Rightly, we enacted laws so people could be fired for treating others unfairly due to their race, gender, religion, sexual orientation and other aspects of their lives. However, think back to those nurses, whose placement of patients on the triage list was biased by their implicit attitudes. Should they be fired for racial prejudice? They might hold strong views on equality, they might have voted for Obama, and they might not even realise they harbour an implicit bias. Are they legally responsible for the biases in their actions that stem from the implicit prejudices they have absorbed from the culture around them? The IAT could be used as a screening tool for hiring nurses and police officers; is that a progressive move, or would it be discriminating against people because of their upbringing?

This question will become more pressing as we measure implicit prejudice more widely. We know that our online words and deeds are tracked obsessively by companies such as Google and Facebook. Equally, they have the technology to measure our implicit behaviours, the timing of our responses and deviations of our clicks. We even wear heart-rate monitors and motion trackers that stream data to a cloud server. All this micro-behavioural data has enormous potential to be mined for insight into implicit attitudes and biases that people may not even know they possess.

Mind vs personality

What makes people different?

Who do you think you are? If you set up a new social media account, you probably have to write a few lines describing yourself. What details do you include? Your job, family, love of small dogs? How do you make it informative, but not too revealing? Perfectly phrased, but also effortless and casual? Regardless, once you have set up such an account, data about you will start to accrue somewhere in the digital cloud. Those digital trackers known as cookies will gather information about where you shop, what news you read and what funny dog videos you like. They're building a picture of who you are, what you like and even how you might vote, then all that information is sold on to advertisers. As we'll see, they can even categorise your personality as accurately as a psychologist, just from your social media feeds. Even though you might agonise over who you are, the cloud knows you very well.

So where did 'you' come from? What made you who you are? In this chapter, we will see how psychologists measure the differences between us; how they take the multifaceted, quirky and special thing that is you, and reduce it to a set of numbers to quantify you scientifically. Once they have something to measure, they can then try to root out the causes and patterns in those numbers. Are they related to the same numbers for your parents, peers or people who went to school with you? Are you purely a product of your genes, your personality created in that first genetic roll of the dice? Or did you emerge from the environment in which you grew, moulded by your experiences?

How do we get the measure of a person? It's a remarkable thing when someone is truly captured by a portrait, a passage in a novel or an impersonation. As scientists, we have to represent people as quantities to capture their essence in numbers. This has happened to you, to some degree, from your schooldays onwards. Each time you took a test, it was an attempt to quantify you – to put a number on your language, reasoning or knowledge. By the time you entered the workplace, you might have been given personality or aptitude tests to place you in the right job, or even to dovetail you with particular colleagues to maximise your teamwork. Along the way, you probably took innumerable personality quizzes in magazines and online, telling you if you're shy or outgoing, a giver or taker in relationships, or which character in the *Harry Potter* novels you most resemble. What is the science behind these ways to quantify us?

Tell me what you see

Let's start with movies. When a bespectacled psychologist interviews someone in a film, they usually bring out

splodgy ink-blot pictures and ask the subject to describe what they see. This is the Rorschach test, and the idea is that in saying what you see in an ambiguous picture – two people hugging, a corpse, two poodles mating – you are revealing something of your inner self. These projective tests are used extensively in the US and Japan. Scientifically speaking, they are almost all nonsense. They tell us very little about a patient, but do reveal quite a bit about the therapist asking the question.

Ink-blot tests are what are known as theory-driven measures. From the work of psychoanalysts such as Sigmund Freud and Carl Jung, psychologists have developed theories about what people might see and what this tells us about them. A patient's responses need to be interpreted in light of those theories and expectations. That's also where the problem lies, because the therapist is more likely than the patient to project their ideas and theories onto the test.

Historically, these tests were often used to 'diagnose' homosexuality, when that was seen as a psychological problem to be fixed. The therapists would be on the lookout for sexual imagery in the patient's responses as an indication of their repressed desires.

In one experiment, gay and straight patients were given the Rorschach test. The gay patients were told to tell the therapist they were gay, but only talk about imagery related to monsters and animals during the test. For example, a patient might have said the ink-blots looked like two elephants fighting. The therapist, with a rich theory about what gay people 'should' see, might note that the patient 'sees elephants, but clearly the trunks are phallic images; reports two hippos but obviously these are buttock substitutes'. According to the therapist's expectations, and from nothing that the patients actually said, the gay patients were diagnosed with repressed sexual imagery. The straight patients, who were told to use sexual imagery, received a different diagnosis. Such projective tests might have a useful function in starting a conversation with a therapist, but they have very little diagnostic value themselves.

More widely used than projective tests are questionnaire measures. Many of these are also theory-driven. For example, a writer for the social news website Buzzfeed may have preconceived ideas about the attributes that determine which *Game of Thrones* character you would be and write questions for a test accordingly. Similarly, using Jungian theories, the psychologists Isabel Briggs Myers and Katharine Cook Briggs developed a personality questionnaire to sort people into different types. According to your answers, you would be categorised as tending towards extraversion or introversion, preferring to use sense or intuition, making decisions through thinking or feeling, and living life by judging or perceiving. The letters of these four categories give you a personality type, such as 'ESTJ'. There are guides as to which jobs would suit you well, which other personality types you might want to date or work with in a team, and even what sort of Christmas present you'd enjoy.

The Myers-Briggs test is the most widely used psychological test of all time. If you work in an office, there's a good chance that you've taken the test. However, you wasted your time. Psychologically, it's meaningless. I would genuinely know more about you scientifically if you told me you were a Lannister or a Stark from *Game of Thrones*. Rather than taking a Myers-Briggs test, it would just as informative, and probably more fun, to have your tea leaves read.

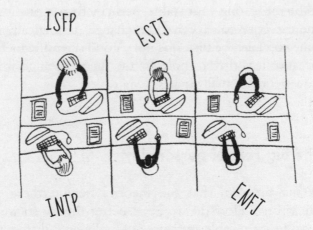

I can be so confidently damning about the test because of solid experimental evidence. The whole idea of it is dubious. We know that whenever we measure something about people, or indeed anything in the natural world, it is normally distributed in a bell curve. This just means that for most things – height, weight, intelligence, a liking for pistachios – most people are lumped in the middle, near the average. The further you get from the average, there are fewer and fewer people. The premise of the Myers-Briggs test is that you split people down the middle into two separate and different categories: thinking or feeling, for example. However, we know that the majority of people are not one or the other, they are right near that border at average.

For this reason and others besides, Myers-Briggs fails an important check of what makes for a good scientific measure. If you take the test a second time, you are fifty per cent likely to get a different answer. It does not have retest reliability. Myers-Briggs is supposed to be measuring your stable, permanent personality, but the category you receive can change dramatically each time you take the test. It is not a good scientific measure because it is driven more by the theory behind it than how people actually behave.

The Big Five of personality

Is the problem that the theories behind these tests are wrong? How do we get a better theory so we can have more reliable measures of individual differences?

Psychologists have come up with an ingenious method in response: to give up on theory.

Empirically driven tests take a dramatically different method. They begin with no theory whatsoever and just hurl a huge number of questions at a huge number of people. For example, they might ask a person to rate if they are relaxed and handle stress well, if they tend to be disorganised, or if they like wavy lines rather than straight. After collecting an enormous number of responses, psychologists employ a mathematical technique called factor analysis. It identifies in the data which questions tend to get similar answers to enable us to discover the latent variables – the hidden factors that predict how people tend to answer.

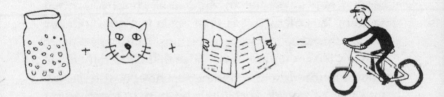

In a survey of attitudes, for example, some people stated that they like lentils, cats and reading about politics. If they gave those answers, they were more likely to enjoy cycling. Another set of people said they liked chips, dogs and reading about celebrity news. They were more likely to follow football. People aren't fully random and there are patterns of answers that go together; factor analysis can identify them. In this particular survey, we know the latent variable, the hidden factor that best predicts the largest number of responses. In this instance, it is whether the respondent reads one of two newspapers:

The Guardian or *The Sun*. I bet you can identify which answers go with which paper, as the responses conform to the stereotypes we have about their readers. Statistically speaking, if we know the single factor of your newspaper of choice, we have a good chance of predicting most of your responses on all the other questions. Of course, it is not perfect, as there are probably chip-eating football fans who read *The Guardian*. Statistically though, that factor is the best predictor.

Factor analysis of personality questionnaires works in the same way. Just looking at the numbers, it tries to identify clusters of questions that go together. Each cluster corresponds to a factor. Not all questions have this quality of patterning with others. If I asked you the second letter of your father's middle name, that is very unlikely to predict anything at all about your other answers. Part of the process of making a questionnaire is then throwing away the questions that don't pattern with any others, and keeping those that pattern together. After a lot of data and number crunching, you end up with a set of questions that reliably pattern together in a small number of clusters.

In the survey of attitudes, there was a factor that predicted most of the responses, which happened to be the newspaper that was read. When the method is applied to personality questionnaires, it has been found that there are about five of these clusters or factors. If someone fills in one questionnaire, we can score them on each of these five factors and predict pretty well their answers to any personality question. It can't be done with a hundred per cent accuracy, but adding in a sixth factor doesn't seem to help very much at all either.

These factors are produced entirely by the data, and no theory goes into the computations. However, looking at what questions are associated with each factor, scientists have given them labels. They are sometimes called the 'Big Five' of personality, and are known collectively as OCEAN: openness to experience, conscientiousness, extraversion, agreeableness and neuroticism. These seem somewhat awkward terms to me. If you asked a priest or a novelist to state the five qualities that make up the human character, I doubt they would end up with these. That said, this is what the data tell us. As far as we can measure it with asking questions, the vast panoply of human variety and personality can be represented by just these five factors.

Politicians with a thousand faces

Now we have a reliable way to quantify human personality, we can see what those numbers predict – quite a lot, as it turns out. There are strong links between personality variables and the objects people keep in their bedrooms and offices, their music collections and their Facebook profile pictures. The World Well-Being Project (WWBP) has given personality tests to a large number of social media users and then analysed all their profile updates and tweets. They found strong connections between the words most commonly used by high-extraversion people ('party', 'baby', 'excited', 'chillin') and by low-extraversion people ('anime', 'computer', 'sigh'); high-openness people ('dream', 'writing', 'music') and low-openness people ('don't', ' :(', 'can't wait').

Since there are predictable links between personality and social media use, this means that someone's public tweets can be used to diagnose their personality. The WWBP asked the permission of participants, as they are responsible scientists; others may have fewer ethical concerns. The American politician Ted Cruz ran in the presidential primaries of 2016. What people signing up for his campaign Facebook page might not have realised is that his staff were data mining their Facebook posts. They then sent campaign messages and ads that were specifically tailored to the personalities of individuals.

Politicians have always bent their messages to suit different audiences, of course. They are two-faced creatures on a professional level. What is different now is the amount of data that we blurt out online and the tools that exist to understand and exploit it. Messages can be tailored not just to groups, such as the working class or retirees, but to individuals. In the digital world, a politician can have a thousand faces, not just two.

Nature or nurture?

We now have the means to quantify personality and put numbers on our individual differences. Aside from

Machiavellian politics, what can we do with this? How can we understand what causes one person to be highly neurotic and another person extraverted? Before the discovery of DNA, before Charles Darwin proposed natural selection and before Gregor Mendel observed differences between pea pods, we were asking how much of our nature comes from our parents and how much from our experience. What has changed now is that we have numbers to give us some answers.

The degree to which your personality (or your intelligence or looks) is defined by your genes, rather than your environment, is called heritability. It's expressed as a number between 1, where the differences in a trait among a population are entirely due to genes, and 0, where the differences are entirely due to the environment or chance. In chapter eight, we'll talk more about how particular situations and environments can determine an individual's behaviour. Here, I want to focus on the genetic side of the equation to understand its role in making us who we are.

To calculate heritability in a single environment amongst a population, you need know two things. First, you need to measure differences in the population – this could be milk yield for cows, or personality or intelligence for people. Second, you need to know how much overlap there is between the genes of the population. This can be calculated from family trees, since we know how much genetic material is shared between twins, siblings and cousins. By looking at these two things – the variability in the measure, and the degree that genes are shared – we can calculate heritability of milk yield, personality or intelligence for that particular environment.

In humans, heritability is 1 for traits that are purely determined by genes (such as eye colour), about 0.7 for weight (a mixture of genes and environment) and 0 for things that are not linked to genes at all (such as the colour of your first car). What about the heritability of psychological attributes? The exact numbers are still hotly contested, as there is always debate over exactly how things should be measured and in what populations. Current estimates are that personality variables such as the Big Five factors have around 0.35 to 0.55 heritability. The condition of schizophrenia, for example, is higher, at around 0.8. Intelligence, the most contested figure, is somewhere between 0.5 and 0.85.

Let's take the higher estimate here and assume that intelligence is a psychological attribute with a heritability of 0.8. That means eighty per cent of your intelligence is due to your biological parents and twenty per cent is due to your upbringing, school, those brain training apps you did for a week, and so on. That places intelligence somewhere between height (0.9) and weight (0.7). So what does that mean?

Does it mean that the difference in standardised test scores between a cash-strapped comprehensive school and a wealthy public school is eighty per cent due to the genetic differences between the parents of the students? Do the public school students do better because they are from better genetic stock? In another example, there is something like a ten per cent difference in standardised intelligence test scores between white and black Americans. Is this difference eighty per cent due to superior genes in the white population? These assertions are readily made by commentators whenever new research on heritability makes the headlines, but are they supported by science?

The clear and unequivocal answer is no. The fact that intelligence is estimated at 0.8 heritability does not at all imply that people from richer schools do better because they were born into more intelligent families, or that differences in achievement between ethnic groups are due to genetics. To state that they are is to fundamentally misunderstand what heritability statistics tell us. It's a frustratingly subtle point, often missed when the science is discussed in the media.

The reason lies in the definition of heritability and how we generalise it. The key point is that heritability is defined and calculated for organisms within the same environment. It cannot be used to generalise between different environments. The reason is that heritability is a proportion of the relative genetic and environmental differences. When the environment changes, so does the heritability proportion.

Imagine some dystopian future where we are all born into identical white boxes, with the same nutrition delivered by tube, and we're nurtured and raised by the same mother-father-teacher wall-sized tablet computer. In this situation, the heritability of intelligence – and all our other traits – would be 1, because by definition our environments are identical. The only way we'd differ would be in our genes, so all the differences between us would be due to genes alone. Genetic mechanisms for personality or intelligence haven't changed, genes don't cause more or less of our brain development, but the environment is the same for everyone. What differences there are between us must be entirely genetic.

Environment

Genes

YOU

The crucial insight is that heritability tells you how much of the variation in a population in a given environment can be explained by genes. Although it seems superficially similar, this is completely different from the statement that genes 'cause' eighty or a hundred per cent of the differences by themselves.

Consider another case. Everyone knows that smoking causes cancer. We can literally see lung cells mutating at a higher rate with each inhalation of smoke. Imagine a world where everyone smokes, all the time, everywhere. Just watch an episode of *Mad Men* or look at clips from the mid-twentieth century. In that toxic world, what factors would decide who gets lung cancer and who doesn't? It would be genes alone, because the presence of cigarette smoke is a constant for everyone. In this scenario, an executive from a tobacco company might say that cigarettes don't cause cancer at all because cancer is just a matter of genetics. They would be comprehensively wrong. Cigarettes would play an equal causal role in the (presumably massive) rates of lung cancer. The heritability of cancer would be high, but that's because the environment would be equally bad for everyone and explains fewer of the differences between people.

Let's return to intelligence. It would only be true that difference in intelligence between white and black Americans is eighty per cent in their genes if those groups had equal environments, equal socioeconomic status and equal opportunities in life. They demonstrably do not. It would only be true that difference in intelligence between children attending rich and poor schools is eighty per cent due to genes if those two environments were identical. They are not.

I know this from personal experience. Eton College is one of the oldest schools in the world. It educates royalty and the wealthy from across the globe. When it was established in the fifteenth century by King Henry VI, it was to educate seventy poor boys. For a short time I was one of those boys. One summer, for two weeks, I was taken from my state comprehensive school and sent to Eton. It was an astonishing experience. I learnt more there in two weeks than in several years at the state school. Every teacher was gifted – that special teacher you might meet once in your life, if you're lucky. The school had its own island. It taught fencing. Admittedly, these skills weren't entirely new to me, as I had already learnt how to fashion a shiv from a broken bottle at my own school. My point is that these were not equal environments.

To take another example, we know that height is very heritable, at 0.9. In fact, most of the time you are the average height of your mother and father, plus a couple of centimetres. In Japan, the average height of the generation born after the Second World War went up by a whole inch. The genetic mechanisms of growth didn't alter, but the diet had changed radically. It was a different environment.

Shaping our futures

Not only do heritability statistics elide the effects of different environments, they give a mistaken view of the causal role of genes. If we think about something that has a relatively high heritability, such as weight (0.7), one could ask what the genes are that account for it. The answer is that we don't yet know. Although we know that some sets of genes account for seventy per cent of variance in weight, we have only identified the individual genes that explain about two per cent. Figuring out the heritability statistics in a given environment and finding the actual genes themselves is almost as big of a leap as figuring out how life could evolve on other planets and actually meeting little green men.

Here's another puzzle that reveals the complexity of the interaction between genes and behaviour. We can calculate heritability statistics for any given psychological trait. We can figure these out for babies, children and adults. So how do they change over a lifetime? You are born a squealing mass of genetic potential. As you age and you have more of life's experiences, does the effect of your environment become more dominant? Do you move away from your genetic heritage and become more a creature of your experience? That would seem a logical conclusion, but it is quite wrong.

Remarkably, as we age and have more experiences, the evidence shows that the heritability of our traits increases. That seems to fly in the face of how we understand the idea of genes and environment. It makes sense once we allow for a simple and reasonable assumption: genes and behaviour interact. When you were a baby, who decorated your nursery? It was probably your parents who picked out the colour scheme. When you were ten years old, perhaps you chose the posters on your bedroom walls. What about when you first left home and were entirely in charge of your space for the first time? What were your decoration choices then?

The point is that as we age, we grow in our ability to shape our own environment. We decorate our own rooms, we choose our own friends, we pick a career and we find someone to spend our lives with. We go to IKEA for the first time and our parents don't pay. Our genes determine how we shape our environment. Aging is one long process of finally getting things just how you like them, and those preferences are largely genetic. As genes can influence what environments are selected, which in turn influences our behaviour, the causal interaction between the two becomes ever harder for scientists to untangle.

None of this says that we are not powerfully determined by our genes, of course. That is not in doubt. It is simply to say that we are only just beginning to understand the causal interaction between genes and behaviour. Heritability statistics, developed to inform farmers' investments, appear an inadequate tool to understand the complex interaction between genes and environment.

Personality vs man

The story of our genes and how they determine us is deeply fascinating and largely unwritten. There is something equally interesting here that we *do* understand on a scientific level – how we reason about each other. Regardless of how genes determine who we are, people reason about each other in very systematic ways. We look at each other's behaviour and assume we are catching a glimpse of the characteristics and nature that let us understand how they'll act in the future. That is a mistake. The science of psychology tells us a different story. What predicts how people will act is not just their personality or genes. Instead, it is often situation that dictates human behaviour. The unseen variable of your culture, job, the people around you and the demands they place on you – all that is simply 'not genetic' in our heritability statistics – has an unacknowledged power over our actions. Everything in our psychology rails against it and wants to assume that it is the character of others that controls their actions. Indeed, there is a psychological reason that people have seized on the heritability statistic and claimed it as evidence for fundamental differences between us. Yet as we shall see, the science of psychology suggests that the difference between ourselves and the other – the murderer, the hero and the coward – can be as slight as the situation in which we find ourselves.

Mind vs actions

Why do people do things?

I have just spent an hour reading the *Daily Mail*, with its celebrities 'flaunting their curves' on the beach or 'hiding their pain' over a break-up. From grainy paparazzi photos, I saw a whole celebrity world of jealousy, pride and plots. Meanwhile, the *Guardian* has images of grim-faced politicians concerned about negotiations or pretending they aren't bothered by poll results. We feel we know these people from the news, that we have insight into the characters of the jilted lovers or struggling leaders. What we don't see is the context of those images. Imagine we could zoom out from those photographs to see the wider frame – the moments before and after. Maybe, like most of us, the beaming grin of the celebrity faded the moment after the snap was taken, or the frown of the politician turned to a smile. They were smiling outside a Starbucks because their drink was refreshing; the politician was grimacing because they had forgotten the PIN code for their phone.

To be, or not to be... in favour of Castro?

When we think about people, we tend to consider their personalities, dispositions and characters. People do the things they do because of who they are. That's the reasoning newspaper writers use, and the rest of us follow. Psychological science shows such reasoning is a fundamental mistake. More often than not, it is the situation people are in that determines their behaviour, not their personality. It is not the actor that produces the drama, it is the stage.

This discovery was made completely by accident. Two psychologists, Edward Jones and Victor Harris, designed an experiment to see how people used behaviour to form impressions of each other. They asked American people to write and then read aloud a political essay, and asked the listening audience to make judgements about the author's views. The study was done in the 1960s, so Jones and Harris asked the participants to write in favour or against the United States' policy toward Cuba and its leader, Fidel Castro – hugely controversial at the time. As expected, the researchers found that the audience thought the author had more left-wing political views if they expressed pro-Castro arguments.

As good scientists, they realised they should have a control condition where the audience was still listening to an argument and evaluating the author, but the essay wasn't really good evidence for their political opinions. In that control condition, the audience was told that the author had no choice in the decision. The experimenters had tossed a coin and told the authors, regardless of personal opinion, to write either a pro- or anti-Castro essay. Here was the surprise result: even when the audience was completely aware the author had been forced to express arguments in favour of Castro, they still judged them to have genuinely pro-Castro views. They failed to take into account the obvious constraints of the situation and falsely concluded that the person's behaviour was caused by their personality and beliefs.

This is not a quirk of that particular experiment. In another experiment, two participants are brought in front of an audience to play a quiz game. The experimenter tosses a coin and makes one a quizmaster, the other a contestant. The quizmaster thinks of half a dozen general knowledge questions to ask the contestant, but is told to make them difficult. The quiz takes place and the audience sees the hapless contestant fail almost every time. The audience is asked to decide which participant is smarter.

Overwhelmingly, they rate the quizmaster as more intelligent. However, we know this is a mistake because the roles were assigned at random by the coin toss. If the experiment is repeated many times, on average the quizmaster and contestant are always going to have about the same level of intelligence. The evidence the audience has for gauging intelligence is clearly useless. The quizmaster is always going to know the answers to all the questions because they made them up in the first place. The structure of the situation means the quizmaster has to get more answers right than the contestant, but people watching the whole experiment ignore all these situational constraints and conclude they are seeing one smart person and one less smart person.

When Americans were polled with the question, 'Who is the smartest person in the country?', many answered that it was Alex Trebek, the host of *Jeopardy!*, a long-running TV game show. In the UK, it seems to be impossible to refer by name alone to Stephen Fry, the former presenter of the panel show *QI*. Instead, he is known as 'brainbox Stephen Fry', 'genius Stephen Fry', or similar. This isn't to say either is unintelligent, it's simply that people who regularly see both men knowing all the answers come to the conclusion that they are seeing geniuses at work. They ignore the fact that they are reading the answers from a card or autocue. We see a complex scenario – but the only explanations we seek are in terms of people, not situations.

Talking to a penguin

The term for this bias in our thinking is the 'fundamental attribution error'. Attributions are the causes we give for people's behaviour. For example, you see a passenger yelling at an airline attendant. You could make the attribution that he is an angry person, which is what we call a dispositional attribution, because it concerns things about him as a person. Or you could assume that the attendant had been rude to the passenger, or that they had lost his luggage, and attribute his behaviour to the situation around him. The fundamental attribution error is that, against the evidence and what can seem like common sense, people make dispositional attributions over situational ones. We tend to blame the person, not the context.

I regularly exploit the fundamental attribution error myself. Like many university lecturers, when I first had to lecture I panicked. I had to speak consistently for an hour to a hundred eager undergrads about a textbook

I hadn't studied since I was an undergraduate myself. They would see right through me. A senior colleague explained I had nothing to fear. 'You don't have to know the whole textbook,' she explained. 'As long as you stay two pages ahead of them, they'll think you know everything.' She was right: the students listened to me speak about a huge range of experiments, answering questions about anything they could think of, and saw an expert in his field. They didn't know those were the *only* studies I knew that were even vaguely related! When I answered one question by saying a writer's work wasn't thematically relevant (because I'd never heard of them), and another by googling the answer in a toilet cubicle during a break, it seemed to them as if I had a world of knowledge at my disposal.

Although it might seem a little sad to think that whatever good opinion my students had of me was mostly due to cognitive error, I find it kind of liberating. It means that we can bluff a lot better than we might imagine. The other day I appeared live on Al-Jazeera discussing the psychology of fake news. I received an email at the last minute asking me to comment on some new research (everyone in my department got the same message, it turned out). I jumped in the cab with my son, who was home from school, and on the way read some Wikipedia articles on the topic in which they wanted me to be an expert. I was led into a dark closet of a room and placed in front of a tiny window with a view of London, into which the camera framed me. I had to talk into the camera, but found it so hard that I got my son to hold up his stuffed penguin toy and talked to that instead. What was shown on TV was an expert in front of a grand London vista; in reality, it was a slightly clueless researcher crouched in a tiny room talking to a penguin. With the fundamental attribution error, no one thinks about the penguin.

The power of the situation

We can see in experiments and everyday life that explanations for people's behaviour revolve around their characters, rather than the situations they're in. Is that really a mistake, though? What evidence is there that the situation really does exert a strong influence over behaviour?

In the aftermath of the Second World War, the scale and horror of the Holocaust became apparent. The Nazis had established a systematic and sickeningly efficient infrastructure dedicated to killing vast numbers of Jewish people, along with other groups. What sort of people could kill so many men, women and children? The world had a chance to find out when some of the perpetrators of the Holocaust were put on trial for their crimes against humanity. In 1961, the German-born Jewish American philosopher Hannah Arendt went to Israel to see the trial of Adolf Eichmann, one of the main officials who implemented the Holocaust. The prosecutor, Gideon Hausner, described Eichmann as uniquely evil and sadistic, saying, 'There was only one man in the satanic structure of Nazism who was almost entirely concerned with the Jews and whose business was their destruction. This was Adolf Eichmann.' Despite this, Arendt described how she saw not a slavering monster filled with hate, but a dull, middle-management civil servant. He was simply following orders, like anyone else does in their job. She called her account of the trial *A Report on the Banality of Evil.*

It has been suggested that the German people had an authoritarian streak; their national character was to obey and follow orders. When a leader like Hitler came to power, they followed his commands, even though they violated every civilised morality. The implication was that in other countries, such as the fiercely independent United States, people would never follow orders in the same way.

Both the claim that Eichmann was a sadist and that the German people are authoritarian are dispositional attributions. They explain the evil of the Holocaust in terms of personality, not situation. American psychologist Stanley Milgram set out to see if they were right – if a holocaust similar to the one organised by the Nazis could only ever happen in a country filled with people of a particular obedient cruelty. His conclusion was published in 1963 and it claimed that in any average town in America, one could easily find sufficient people to carry out acts of terror and genocide. This is not a conclusion about the fundamental evil character of humanity, it is a statement of the power of the situation.

Milgram set up an experiment designed to get people to rebel. He wanted to put people in a situation where they were asked to perform a series of increasingly horrible acts so he could measure the point at which they stood up to authority. In a sense, he failed.

Participants thought they had been recruited to take part in an experiment on learning. They arrived at Milgram's laboratory at the prestigious Yale University to meet the experimenters and another person who was to take part in the experiment. They tossed a coin and one person was given the role of the learner, the other the role of teacher. The coin toss was faked, so the only real participant was the person given the role of teacher, while the learner was an actor. The participant was told that the experiment was looking at the effect of punishment on learning, which was a plausible study for the time. The teacher was told to read out a list of word pairs that the learner had to memorise. The teacher then read out a word and the learner had to say its paired word. If a mistake was made, the teacher had to press a button to administer an electric shock to the learner.

The teacher was told that with each incorrect response they should increase the voltage of the shock. The lightest shock was 15 volts, which increased by 15 volts each time all the way to 450 volts. There were labels describing what these numbers meant, such as 'slight shock', 'strong shock' and 'danger – severe shock'. The final two switches, for 435 and 450 volts, were labelled

'XXX' in red. What Milgram wanted to know was at what point the participant would decide this was too much pain to deliver to an innocent person.

Teacher and learner were placed in different rooms and communicated via an intercom. In reality, the learner's responses were pre-recorded to follow a script. At around 75 volts, the teacher heard the learner grunt in pain. At 120 volts, the learner yelled. At 150 volts, they screamed that they wanted to leave the room, that they had a heart condition and needed to leave the experiment. If the teacher asked to stop, the experimenter monitoring the scenario told the teacher that the experiment required them to continue. At 285 volts, the learner screamed hysterically. After 300 volts, the teacher heard something worse: complete silence. At this point, the teacher believed they were administering a highly painful electric shock to another human being with a heart condition, who was probably unconscious and possibly dead. The experimenter asked them to continue.

How many people do you think would continue all the way to the 450-volt shock? Note that the teacher wasn't being threatened or rewarded at all. If you were in this situation, at what point do you think that you would have stopped and refused to carry on?

When Milgram explained the experiment to his colleagues, they predicted that only one per cent of the population would deliver the highest volt. Only a rare type of person – an authoritarian or a sadist, perhaps – would cause that much pain to another person. Milgram himself predicted that most people would rebel. I would guess that you imagine you aren't the sort of person who would obey those orders either. However, such predictions make the fundamental attribution error. They imagine that behaviour would be caused by a person's disposition and they underestimate the power of Milgram's situation.

In fact, *sixty-three per cent* of participants administered the very highest shock of 450 volts. The average stopping point was 360 volts, after the learner had supposedly lost consciousness. Milgram repeated the experiment many times, with men and women from different parts of the world, and found consistent results. Repeating the experiment today is difficult, as it breaks many of our guidelines on ethical research, but it was replicated by my colleagues at University College London using a virtual reality learner. It was also recently recreated for TV, because TV has far fewer ethical guidelines than science. The results are the same today: most people would administer lethal shocks to an innocent person.

However, those people do not do so quietly. Footage of the original experiment or the subsequent replications shows the teachers are in turmoil. They ask the experimenter repeatedly if everything is OK and if the learner needs help. They plead with the learner to get the answer right. They say that they think what is happening is wrong. Despite this, they keep going. All it takes is a person in a white lab coat to give them orders and they obey. It was this result that led Milgram to the conclusion that there would be enough foot soldiers to carry out a similar event to the Holocaust in any mid-sized American town.

These results also enabled Milgram to reject the personality explanation for the Holocaust. It's probably not that there is something different about the German character, but it was the situation that compelled them to act. In that case, what is it that is so powerful about the situation?

Milgram explored this by modifying the situation and measuring how participants' obedience changed. He found that many factors contributed to the authority of the scientists. If they moved the location of the experiment from the august campus of Yale University to some rundown offices, obedience dropped. If there were two experimenters and the teacher heard them arguing with each other, they were more likely to disobey. If the teacher was placed in the same room as the learner and had to physically place their hand on the electrode, they stopped sooner. In other words, it's easier to hurt others when they are distant and when ordered by people with the trappings of authority and unity.

We can see these factors at work today. The military rigorously adheres to a strict uniform code, even when far from a battlefield. There is no practical value to dressing in camouflage gear, for example, but there is a great psychological value in inducing obedience by marking out clearly who has authority. We have the technology to create enormous distances between ourselves and the consequences of our acts. A drone can be piloted thousands of miles from the scene of its kill; the results resembling little more than a battle on a games console.

Psychological distance and the appearance of authority are striking features of the situation that Milgram set up, but one of the most powerful aspects of his experiment was more innocuous: the design of the electrocution box. Milgram concluded that the fact that the volts gradually increased put people in a situation where, psychologically, it made it very hard to stop.

Participants in the experiment had to weigh two things against each other: they were asked by an authority figure to cause harm, but causing harm to others is bad. When the voltage is low, a tickle of 15 volts, that seemed like an easy calculation. Obeying authority and contributing to a scientific experiment seemed like a good trade-off. The same went for 30 and 45 volts. At what voltage did the principle of doing no harm become more important than science? These are two abstract principles that are hard to square philosophically, let alone translate into an exact number of volts.

There's another problem. Say at 270 volts a teacher decided it was wrong to cause harm to another person, regardless of what the scientist said. If it was wrong at 270 volts, then it was probably wrong at 255, 240 and 225 volts as well. In other words, for the teacher to stop at one particular point was to imply they had been doing the wrong thing all along. As we saw in chapter three, people do not like to feel that they are in the wrong. It causes cognitive dissonance, and people will contort themselves psychologically to avoid it. They will justify their actions in all sorts of ways, rather than admit that they have done wrong. This is the 'foot-in-the-door' technique that we discussed before. If you want to get someone to do something evil or against their nature, then gradually escalate your demands and they justify their actions for you.

The prison experiment

Obedience to authority is just one way in which the situation can drive behaviour, of course. The Stanford University prison experiment of 1971 is another shocking example of the power of the situation, and is another experiment that we don't do today because of ethical concerns (although it has also been recreated on TV).

One summer, psychology professor Philip Zimbardo recruited a selection of young, college-age men to take part in his experiment, screening them to be sure they weren't susceptible to mental illness. At the start of the study, he tossed a coin. It is from that random coin toss, and nothing about the participants' personalities, that everything followed. According to the result, half the participants were designated as guards, the other half as prisoners. They were taken to a mock jail that Zimbardo had created in the basement of the psychology department at Stanford University. The guards were given the job of keeping order, the prisoners the job of being imprisoned, and everyone was paid $15 a day to play along.

Things began jovially enough, with the prisoners joking and resisting the guards' attempts to boss them about. The guards began taking steps to break up the camaraderie, setting up a privilege cell with better food and bedding, and an isolation cell with no sheets. They turned the prisoners against each other, asking them to choose who to victimise. They started to wake the prisoners at random intervals in the night to humiliate them with petty punishments. Within a few days, all of the participants had taken on their roles to a frightening extent. One of the guards had adopted a swagger (they called him 'John Wayne') and took particular pleasure in exercising his cruelty.

A priest who worked at a real prison was asked to visit the pretend prisoners. He was astonished when the prisoners gave their inmate numbers rather than their names. There was a threat of a riot, to which the guards responded by increasing their abuse. Prisoner 416 refused to eat his food in protest and was thrown into a cell, while the guards told the other prisoners to shout insults at him. The guards gave the other prisoners a choice: if they wanted, they could allow 416 to have one of their blankets. No one donated their bedding, so he spent the night shivering in solitary confinement.

After a few short days, this area of the psychology department had become a place of hysterical sobbing, cruelty and institutional abuse. I worked at Stanford thirty years after the study, but after watching the footage I always avoided that basement.

What created this situation? Think back to the coin toss and that moment of random assignment. There were no personality differences, on average, between the prisoners and the guards. The only difference between these people was the situation in which they were placed: prisoner or guard.

We all act in a certain way depending on a situation. In a church, pub or hospital, there are very different ways of speaking and behaving that we immediately adopt. When a waiter brings wine to your table, you taste it to check it isn't corked. This little scene is played out countless times, even though it is usually entirely pointless because these days many wines have either synthetic corks or screw-tops. We persist in the ritual because it's how you behave in restaurants. Participants in the Stanford prison experiment knew how guards and prisoners were supposed to act. All it took was the right costume to perform the roles.

It's all about the money

The experiments we've discussed are extreme examples, so let's end with one final example where behaviour can be explained better by situation than disposition.

I'll begin with an assertion: rich people are arseholes. That might seem like some form of prejudice (and, in part, it is), but there is actually scientific evidence behind it. Imagine you're walking and come up to a zebra crossing. You haven't set your foot on the road, but are just about to. A car is approaching and the driver has to make a decision: do they speed up to go over the crossing before you get to it, or do they politely slow down and stop, anticipating your need to cross? If the car is an expensive SUV, do you think the driver is more likely to speed up or slow down?

Psychology professor Paul Piff and his colleagues collected data on this very question, standing on the streets of a Californian town to note when drivers slowed down or sped up, recording the cars' make and model. They estimated the cost of these cars and found a clear relationship: the more expensive the car, the more likely the driver is to accelerate to stop the pedestrian crossing. So, rich people are arseholes.

Now that's a dispositional attribution, of course. I'm claiming that richer people, who drive more expensive cars, are a particular type of person. Maybe to get rich, you have to be a bit selfish, willing to take risks and seize opportunities. This brings you financial success in life, but also makes you a bit of a dick behind the wheel. Piff has explored another possibility: perhaps it's the situation. Money makes people selfish.

Piff was able to show this experimentally, at least with toy money. In one of his studies, people played the board game *Monopoly*. The experimenters literally stacked the deck so some people ended the game with a big pile of money, while others did not. Then the experimenter made excuses to leave the room. As they left, they pointed to a bowl of sweets on the table and told the participant to help themselves. They also explained that the sweets were meant for some children who were coming to play the game later. Then they shut the door. Returning after the participant had left, the experimenters found that those who ended the game with more money helped themselves to more sweets. They took candy from babies.

Many other experiments have shown that when people are induced to feel rich or powerful, it changes how they think. There are many ways to do this, but it can be as simple as asking people to remember a time they fired someone, or a time that they were fired. Then you can ask people to search for a target object amongst a field of distractors, or to make decisions about job candidates. What you find is that people who feel more powerful have a narrower attention window. They are slower at searching for things on screen than people who feel less powerful. Those who feel powerful are more likely to follow their intuition than external information. They are also more likely to be biased in their thinking and judge people based on social stereotypes about race and gender, rather than facts on a CV.

How to explain success

In all these experiments, we are not showing that people in different positions in society have different personalities and behave in different ways. We are taking a set of participants, randomly making them feel either powerful or powerless, and showing that those situational factors change how they behave.

Despite all the evidence of social psychology, our thinking is dominated by the fundamental attribution error: we want to describe everything in terms of personalities. This has profound effects on the structure of our society. We look at people who end up with wealth and power and ask what accounts for their success.

We look at someone such as the billionaire Bill Gates and call him a genius for creating the personal computer revolution. As the writer Malcolm Gladwell argues, what we don't think about is the luck and opportunity that he had in going to a highly privileged school, one of the few in the world that had a computer, which he was allowed to play with. We revere the talent and uniqueness of professional athletes, ignoring the good fortune that often distinguishes them from their non-professional peers. Two-thirds of Canadian professional hockey players were born in January or February, for example, meaning that they were slightly more grown than their peers of the same year. We don't think of these situational, random constraints, we just see winners and assume there is something special about them.

What about the unsuccessful? Why did their lives end up like that? We tend to think it's because they are lazy, unfit or simply untalented. We attribute and explain each other's position in life in terms of personality. This is not to say that individual differences in talent and motivation do not play a huge role, but whatever influence there is as a result of situation in determining someone's path, we are psychologically blind to it. We tend to underestimate the importance and the causal role of differences in upbringing, schooling or opportunity. It makes a progressive, egalitarian and fair society very hard to achieve when we believe secretly that success comes from 'magical' qualities. The evidence from psychology is that we overlook the powerful and pervasive influence of the situation of our lives to tell stories of characters, heroes and villains instead.

Actions vs man

I cannot think of a more dominant personality in my lifetime than President Donald J Trump. What I mean is that we feel we know more about his personality than anyone else. In psychology, there is something called the Goldwater rule. It is a principle agreed by the profession that clinical psychologists should never diagnose people who are in the public eye without a proper assessment, as it would degrade professional standards to offer opinions. However, a large group of my colleagues signed a letter arguing that in the case of Trump, the Goldwater rule should be suspended as he is a clinical narcissist who should not be allowed power.

As hard as this is to say, maybe we are too harsh on Trump. Or rather, perhaps we too have fallen into the fundamental attribution error of assuming that all of his behaviour stems from his pure 'Donald Trumpness'. There is a situation that has produced and supported the man we see; a lifetime of wealth and privilege, of only meeting poor people when it is their job to serve him. No one buys into the myth of Donald J Trump more than Donald J Trump himself. When questioned about money he acquired from his father's estate, he stated in a deposition that it was 'a very small amount ... I think it was like in the $9 million range'. Wealth beyond most of our dreams is negligible to him. Rather than thinking of his behaviour as the actions of a delusional narcissist, think of thcm as the actions of a man born and nurtured with the trappings of power.

I am not pleading for you to have sympathy for Trump. I am suggesting that the key to understanding how he got power (and how he might eventually lose it) will not be found in the endless personality profiles we read in newspapers. It's in understanding the complex social forces that produced his behaviour, and more importantly, the behaviour of people who voted for him. It might be easy for his opponents to say that Trump is racist and sexist, therefore so is everyone who voted for him. However, this analysis by disposition is overlooking the true psychological causation behind Trump and his supporters. Remember that an hour or so of playing *Monopoly* and winning all that money turned participants into people who took sweets from children. Consider what a lifetime of being Donald J Trump has done to him. The evidence is that with a bit more money in your pocket, you'd also become a bit more like Trump.

With more money in your pocket, you might behave a little more like Trump

Mind vs the supernatural

Why do we see ghosts?

Britain is becoming a godless place. Though the majority of us now declare that we have no religion at all, it would seem that we are less willing to give up on the supernatural. Depending on the question, somewhere between a third and a half of people have some sort of belief in spirits, ghosts and hauntings. One in ten claims to have seen a ghost or contacted the dead. In this chapter, we will explore why this is. Understanding the reasons for believing in ghosts will reveal little about the supernatural realm, but will unlock insights into how we perceive, interpret and recall the world around us.

To frame our scientific discussion, I want to describe some documentary footage that I think captures the phenomenon. The film begins with an old Victorian house with gothic architecture. It's night and the moon is up. Suddenly, bats screech across the sky. Scenes now appear in a quick montage. We see a group of five walking across the screen, their long shadows stretching before them. Now there are shapes of other people, hands and faces in the corners of rooms, floating eerily. The five get scared and start running. Then we see a quick series of skulls, suits of armour and glowing eyes. One of the five, a man with red hair, is particularly scared. The group walks past an old portrait, and the eyes in the painting follow them. They're all terrified now, and the red-haired man jumps into the arms of his dog, who then licks a pink substance – perhaps ice cream – off his own head. The video ends with the plaintive cry, 'Scooby, Scooby-Doo, where are you?'

The footage is the title sequence of the Hanna-Barbera cartoon from my childhood. You can see many videos of supposedly real supernatural encounters on YouTube, but I would argue that the title sequence of *Scooby-Doo* is a remarkable distillation of our cultural knowledge about ghosts. In under a minute, it contains a huge number of the key features of ghost stories and experiences, from the tales of Edgar Allan Poe to the movie *Poltergeist*.

To clarify, I am not trying to debunk particular cases of supposed happenings or using science to answer the question of whether ghosts exist. On balance, I think that ghosts do not exist in any form. Then again, I am a typical atheist, a sceptical scientist with no soul – exactly the type that tends to be killed off in the second act of most horror stories. In contrast, you might have some sort of belief in the afterlife. There is nothing in this chapter that will try to disabuse you of that.

It is the common features of ghost stories and experiences of the sort captured by *Scooby-Doo* that we are going to try and explain in this chapter. Where do they happen? In what environment and under which conditions? If you asked a dozen people to write the first paragraph of a typical ghost story, I would predict they would all look pretty similar. Is that simply because we all watched *Scooby-Doo* as kids, or are there deeper psychological reasons for the times and places haunted by 'typical' ghosts?

In our answer, we will draw on many of the features and mechanisms of the brain that we have discussed elsewhere in this book. We'll track how a simple illusion in perception can become entrenched in memory, gaining certainty with each retelling. This psychological process – from mistake to confident, fervent belief – characterises not just the supernatural, but many of our beliefs about the world and our own history.

Who turned out the lights?

We could think of being in a haunted house as a set of perceptual experiences. If so, what are their relevant psychological features? Haunted places are usually unfamiliar locations you wouldn't typically experience, such as old mansions. Also, you are probably there at an unusual time, such as the dead of night. There might be only flickering candles for light, with perhaps a lightning storm outside. There are strange noises. Old houses creak with arthritic floorboards and rusty hinges. The wind makes howling noises down the chimney.

All of this adds up to two things: unfamiliarity and ambiguity. In a haunted house, you experience things you rarely see, in a different context, and can't quickly explain. Your perceptual system does not like this. As we have seen elsewhere in this book, it functions to give you answers, to deliver an interpretation of the world around you without ambiguity. It does this by building up experience of the world, by learning from familiar things. Unfamiliarity and ambiguity are the mortal enemies of your perceptual system. Often, your mind responds to these conditions by leaping to an interpretation based on its expectations.

We can examine ambiguous stimuli in simple lab experiments to see how they can be interpreted in one way or another. For example, you can ask people what the word 'bark' means, but flash them the word 'dog' or the word 'tree' moments before. Reliably, this little nudge – called a 'prime' in experimental psychology – will push people towards the interpretation of the word as the sound of an animal or the skin of a tree accordingly.

Primed perceptions become part of a memory. You can show people two circles connected by a line and ask them to remember the image. Beforehand, you can prime them with the word 'glasses' or 'barbell'. Later, they will tend to redraw those pictures either with a little bend in the line between, as if bridging a nose in a pair of spectacles, or with two lines, showing a bar connecting two weights. Once the mind has settled on an interpretation of an ambiguous stimulus, it can be quite difficult to shake.

Back to the haunted house. The likelihood is that you are not there by chance. You were dared to spend a night in the creepy mansion. There are tales of people who died there. Perhaps there is a plaque somewhere telling the legend of a ghost that walks the halls. Maybe everyone keeps themselves awake that night by telling ghost stories.

The point is that in the context of a haunted house, with all its ambiguity, creaks and howls, the situation will

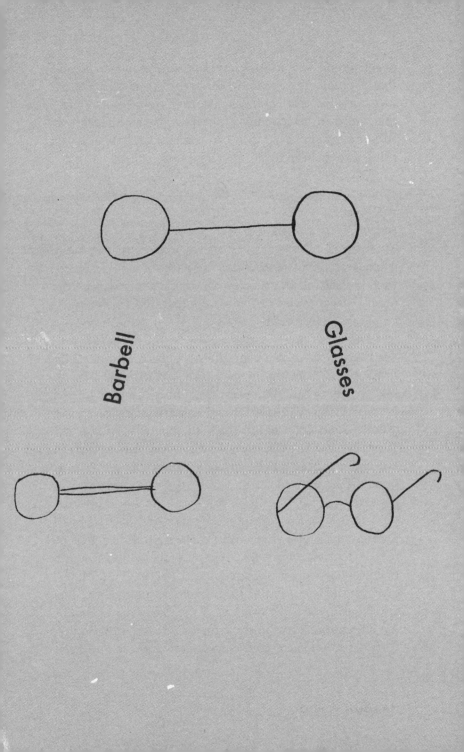

Barbell

Glasses

have primed you to expect the supernatural. You'll be thinking, talking or reading about ghosts at the moment you perceive that stimulus. At that point, you'd utter the line from every ghost movie in a trembling voice: 'What was that?' Your mind will answer with what it was primed to answer all along: it was a ghost.

Mona Lisa's eyes

There weren't just creaks and howls in *Scooby-Doo*. There were ghostly faces, floating spookily. Once again, the precise environment of a typical haunted house could create that experience.

Think of fog, floating eerily, lit by the moon. As you'll know if you've ever laid on grass and looked up at clouds, water vapour can take on different shapes and forms at random. Your perceptual system suffers from the phenomenon we discussed in chapter two, called pareidolia: the tendency to see faces in objects. It might be that there are some faces already lurking in our hypothetical, stereotypical haunted house, such as portraits and stone busts. Could they be perceived as ghosts?

I once viewed some cave art that had puzzled archaeologists. It was a picture of a buffalo with eight legs. It wasn't a 'spider-buffalo', more that the animal seemed to have been drawn twice on top of itself. However, when the archaeologists lit the image by candlelight, they saw what the artist had done. A flickering flame caught the uneven surfaces of the cave wall at different angles. What they saw was one four-legged buffalo, and then the other, flicking back and forth as they were caught by the flame. The buffalo was running. Amazingly, this was deliberate artistic animation 40,000 years before Disney.

In a draughty haunted house lit by a candle flickering from the wind outside, it is possible that a similar effect could occur by accident, rather than artistic design. Someone could mistake the motion of the flame that is lighting a face as motion of the face itself.

There is another way that faces can move, or at least their eyes. As you may have experienced, if a face is painted with the eyes looking directly at the viewer, those eyes seem to move around as the viewer shifts, always fixating on them. And there is another visual illusion that can produce this perception. In chapter two we talked about foveal and peripheral vision. Due to the way photoreceptors are clustered at the back of the eyeball in the fovea, the centre of your vision, you are sensitive to things with high spatial frequency. This means small-scale, high-contrast differences, such as letters on a page. In your periphery, you cannot perceive fine detail. Instead, you are sensitive to low spatial frequencies, larger blobs and patterns of light and dark.

This mechanical difference in your eyeball could be responsible for one of the most famous features of Western art: the enigma of *Mona Lisa*'s smile. That's the hypothesis of neurobiologist Margaret Livingstone. She processed da Vinci's painting with a computer algorithm to show only low spatial frequencies. The result looks a bit like a blurry, low-resolution version, as if you're squinting at an old computer graphic of the portrait. In this image, there are shadows under each cheekbone that give *Mona Lisa* the appearance of having a warm smile. Then Livingstone processed the painting to show only the high spatial frequencies. The result looks a bit like someone has traced the painting with a thin pencil, as it shows only the fine detail and none of the shadow and shade. What dominates here is the narrow line of *Mona Lisa*'s mouth separating her lips. The curve is flat, and while not quite a frown, it is an underwhelmed and forced smile at best.

Livingstone's hypothesis is that you perceive a different emotion in *Mona Lisa*'s face depending on where you are looking at her. As you look at the portrait, your gaze moves all the time. If you look into *Mona Lisa*'s eyes, then her mouth is in your peripheral vision and looks as if it is happy and welcoming. If you look closer, then her mouth is in your high spatial frequency, central vision, and her smile has turned sour and disapproving. You look back at her eyes, and she smiles at you once more.

This is why people spend so long looking at the *Mona Lisa*, tricked by that turncoat smile. Remarkably, there is some evidence that da Vinci painted this effect deliberately. At least, it seems he built up the portrait in layers, painting the detailed, frowning version on top of the smiling low-frequency version, like the galloping buffalo created by the cave painters.

A similar illusion could be seen in our haunted house. Think of a portrait of a person facing the front, their eyes looking to the left. Typically, a painter might draw small, high-contrast dots for the pupils in the left-hand corner of the eye. On the right of the eyeballs, there might be painted some shadow to show their roundedness. Just like the *Mona Lisa*, these two features will stand out differently to central and peripheral vision. When a viewer looks directly at the eyes, the detailed pupils will pop out and the face will look to the left. With peripheral vision, those shadows on the right-hand side of the eyeballs will dominate and look like pupils, and the face will look to the right. If the portrait is painted in a particular way, it is possible that the eyes of a face will dart from one side to another as you look across the canvas. When you look directly at the face, it will be still.

Like a devious schoolchild, only when you look away will it sneak a glance in the other direction.

Poltergeists on the move

Ghosts are not stuck in picture frames, though, they float about and walk through walls. How can that be a visual illusion? The faces on display have one more trick to play in our haunted house. Remember that it is usually a dark and stormy night in our stereotypical ghost story. It's possible that the weather could interact with faces to explain the precise nature of spectral appearances.

Make sure you are in plenty of light, then take a look at the blotchy image on this page. Pick one spot on the image and stare at it for between thirty seconds to a minute without moving your eyes. Try to sing the whole of the *Scooby-Doo* theme tune and that'll be about the right timing. When you're done, look immediately at a blank white surface, such as a table or wall, and try to notice as much as you can about your phenomenological experience.

What did you see? If you are like most people, you'll say 'Jesus', or 'some generic hippy'. This is an example of an after-image. What you see is a sort of colour inversion of the original image, which appears when you look away to the blank surface. It's usually a bit blurry around the edges. You may have experienced an after-image demonstration; you'll certainly have experienced them when someone has let off a flash from a camera directly into your eye, or you've accidentally looked at the sun or directly into some headlights. (Isaac Newton was obsessed by these after-images and used to produce them by hooking a bodkin – a big needle – into his eye socket and prodding his retina. Needless to say, this is hugely dangerous and should never be attempted.)

In all of these cases, the cells in your eye that are sensitive to one particular colour become overstimulated and fatigued. They get tired of sending out the same signal in response to exactly the same stimulus. This rarely happens in everyday life, as you are continually moving your eyes and providing different levels of stimulation to each individual cell. However, when you artificially keep your eyes very still for a long time, or your eyes are flooded with a really intense light in one instant, those cells will be knocked out for a short while.

Say you were looking at bright red circle for a long time, or a car's break lights in the dark. When you look away from the image to a blank surface, the cells responding to red continue to be fatigued and will give out an artificially low response. However, the cells that respond to the opposite colour (green, since you were looking at red) are just fine and respond at their regular rate. To figure out the colour you see, the brain compares the activity of the red cells versus the green cells, in what's called 'opponent processing'. Since the tired red cells have a lower response, the brain now sees green in exactly the areas where the cells saw red, for at least a few seconds until the red cells get their strength back. At that point, the after-image fades away. After-images are related to a broad class of phenomena called adaptation, where the brain ceases or reduces its response to constant stimuli. If the stimuli are suddenly removed, then often some sort of after-effect is produced.

Let's return to the face after-image. You might have noticed something else peculiar about the hippy face. It is burnt on to a particular spot on your retina, so wherever you look, the after-image will appear. This has two consequences. Firstly, if you look from a page that is close to you to a wall across the room, the image will appear much bigger. It's taking up the same spot on your retina, but just like a movie projector, it will scale up to a larger size with surfaces further away. Secondly, the after-image will move whenever you move your eyes, as that retinal spot is also moving around. The image can shoot from one side of the room to the other if you move your eyes quickly, or stay in the same spot if you fixate on a wall. People are largely unaware of the degree to which they move their eyes around, so as a retina image bobs and floats, people feel as if it is moving by itself and not moved by their own eye movements.

After-images are face-like fuzzy images that exist for only a few seconds, can appear larger than life, float around, can move very fast, then suddenly disappear. Remind you of anything? They're produced by staring at a face for a long time – which doesn't usually happen outside of a psychology demonstration – or they can happen if it is dark and you are looking at an image of a face that is suddenly lit by an intense burst of light. Such as lightning on a dark and stormy night while looking at a portrait.

The exact, and perhaps only, natural conditions that can produce a spontaneous face after-image are exactly the conditions that occur in a stereotypical haunted house. The properties of ghosts in stories and *Scooby-Doo* – their fuzzy appearance, movement and sudden disappearance – match exactly the properties of visual after-images. I don't think these are coincidences.

Flashbulb moments

There is one final aspect of ghost stories that is absolutely vital in inculcating a belief in the supernatural. Ghost stories are stories. They are told and retold. It is the retelling, around a campfire, each Halloween, during horror movie marathons, that is a vital part of their psychological power.

We often think of memory like a recording. Our eyes are the camera and the brain is the videotape, hard drive or memory card that stores what we perceive and replays when we recollect. We saw earlier that this common metaphor for the eye as a camera is remarkably misleading, as is the idea of memory as a recorder. Instead, remembering is more like a retelling a story.

There are significant moments in time that we share with other people, moments when our stories connect with a bigger narrative. These are called flashbulb memories. The term comes from old newsreels in which you could see a moment, such as a celebrity being led to a police car or a politician resigning, lit up by the flashing lightbulb of the photographers. People said that everyone knew where they were when they heard JFK had died; you could substitute that for any flashbulb memory event.

In 1988, the late cognitive psychologist Ulric Neisser decided to test his students' flashbulb memory for a significant event in their lives: the Challenger space shuttle disaster. It was two and a half years after the event, and Neisser asked participants to recollect what they were doing the moment they heard that the space shuttle had exploded shortly after take-off.

> 'When I first heard about the explosion I was sitting in my freshman dorm room with my roommate and we were watching TV,' recalled one student. 'It came on a news flash and we were both totally shocked. I was really upset and I went upstairs to talk to a friend of mine and then I called my parents.'

This is a classic flashbulb memory. Could you recall what you were doing on this day two and a half years ago with such a level of detail? The chances are that you cannot, but this participant has a rich, detailed memory as if it were yesterday. That flashbulb had burnt the details into the student's memory.

However, that memory is a lie; it's not what happened to that person on that day. How can we be so certain? In 1986, the day after the Challenger disaster, Neisser had asked students in his class to write down exactly what they were doing when they had heard the news. In 1988, he found the students who had responded and asked them again for their 'flashbulb memories'. This is what that same student wrote the day after the disaster:

> 'I was in religion class and some people walked in and started talking about [it]. I didn't know any details except that it had exploded and the schoolteacher's students had all been watching which I thought was so sad. Then after class I went to my room and watched the TV program talking about it and I got all the details from that.'

It looks like the memory of a completely different person, yet they were written by the same person, in the same handwriting. This student was not unusual in this failing of memory. A quarter of the recollections in 1988 were wrong about every single detail mentioned: where they were when they heard, what their reaction was, what they did next, and so on. Half the people were wrong about at least two-thirds of their memories. Only seven per cent of the respondents remembered what actually happened to them.

Here's the key thing about this experiment: Neisser asked how confident people were in their memories. Perhaps people had no idea, just as you might have no recollection of what you were doing on this day two and a half years ago. Perhaps those statistics are just the rates you get for guessing. However, many people were absolutely certain of their memories for that day; others were less so. Crucially, there was no correlation between people's certainty about their memories and their actual accuracy. It's what you would expect if people were guessing, but these people weren't. This is systematic memory failure.

Where does the memory distortion come from? It's the retelling of the story. The key point is that these flashbulb memories are things we talk about after the event: in the moments immediately following it, in the weeks after, reflecting back at New Year's Eve parties and reminiscing years later. Each time the story is retold, it is reconstructed from a partial memory at the time, TV footage seen later, someone else's story that was overheard, and so on. The memory is reconstructed each time from slightly different materials.

Many people in the US remember seeing on live TV the first plane hitting the Twin Towers in 2001. George W Bush, the president at the time, recalls watching it on TV. Donald Trump, the president at the time of writing, remembers crowds of Muslim people celebrating in New Jersey. Neither of these things happened. The first crash wasn't shown live at all; footage of that event was found and broadcast later on, which was then incorporated into people's sincerely held memories of the event.

It is not only huge news events that are subject to this distortion. All memory works this way. A favourite family anecdote is about a time I cut my thumb. I was about five years old and we were at the beach. I was playing with one of those collapsible deckchairs and it collapsed. It pinched and split my thumb open. I started to run around in circles screaming and shaking my hand over my head. Blood hosed out of my thumb, splattering the faces of every family member in the vicinity. No one could catch me, let alone stop the bleeding. I can see my granny's face and hair covered in blood spray; I can see my brother's ice cream cone dripping in red; I can remember the droplets of blood landing on the beach and congealing with the sand, caking the outside. Then, a passing lady who happened to be a nurse walked up to me very calmly, grabbed my thumb firmly and held it until the bleeding stopped.

This was a long time ago and I no longer run around spraying people with blood when I get a cut. Still, every time there's a minor injury or slip of a kitchen knife at home, someone will tell the injured person not to be like me and stand still.

A few years ago, following another kitchen incident, I asked my father if it was on the Isle of Wight where I cut my thumb. He looked at me blankly, so I recounted the memory I've just described. He shook his head. I *had* cut my thumb around that age, but we weren't at the beach. I had found some deckchairs in the garage and was playing with them. There was a lot of blood that went everywhere and I wouldn't stand still. There was no passing nurse, but a neighbour who was medically trained helped to bandage me.

Almost every detail of my memory (which still feels accurate) was false. There was no blood splattered on granny's face, no sand, no bleeding ice cream. It was all a fiction I had spun based on the fact that deckchairs were involved. When I look back, the beach in my memory does seem too picture-postcard. The deckchairs are the old-fashioned type you don't see any more. I had grabbed these images from elsewhere and built them into my memory each time the family retold the tale. I inspected my memory of the passing nurse and realised she was wearing a blue dress, black hat and a sort of bustle thing. I had inserted Mary Poppins into my childhood recollection. Hearing about some helpful, competent woman, that was the visual image I had brought in to form my memory.

Even now, knowing that it is mostly a fiction, that moment on the beach still feels like my memory. It seems as real to me as other childhood moments, such as a birthday or the first day of school. The chances are that your flashbulb memories of your past, your recollection of family stories told and retold, will be just as fictional and fabricated as mine. We are not all fantasists, this is just how memory works.

Think back to those ghostly experiences. They're good stories. From the moment they are experienced, they are retold among the people who were there, then with their friends, then with their family. Each time they are retold, they are reconstructed from things that did happen, things that maybe did not happen, or things that were actually seen by someone else. The ambiguity, doubt and things that didn't fit get dropped to make room for a better story. In all the time of retelling, it seems like a genuine memory. The fictions and embellishments don't subtract from its veracity, they make it seem more vivid and true. I think that is the essence of why people believe in ghosts.

The supernatural vs man

This chapter is not just about supernatural experiences; more broadly, it's about the fact that what we experience is what we interpret the world to be, and how that influences the stories we tell each other afterwards. Our perceptual system is not built to accurately perceive the world, and our memory is not there to faithfully record it. We interpret and guess at the time, then we embellish and confabulate later. This is not a function of people's deceitfulness, egoism or self-aggrandisement. It is simply how we are built. This is vital to understand when we try and separate fact from gossip, fake news from real news, or weigh up eyewitness testimony. It is important, not just in reassuring ourselves late at night that the ghost story we heard is just fiction, but in judging the objective truth of the experiences of others and separating it from the sincerity of their memory.

Conclusion

The story of *Man vs Mind* has an odd history. There's a hole in the plot. On the one hand, the understanding of our own thoughts and behaviour is some of the oldest wisdom we have. *The Epic of Gilgamesh*, one of humanity's earliest surviving stories, is rich with the psychological intrigues of envy, pride and love. Religious scripture – the Vedas, Bible, Koran and Torah – are as much guidebooks to our own daily thought and behaviour as they are descriptions of things spiritual. There is a long-abiding curiosity in the human mind, but this does not sit well with another fact: psychology is a remarkably young science.

Around 500 years ago, we invented the scientific method, which is the most successful way we have found to accumulate knowledge of the world around us. It led to runaway intellectual progress that brought us the Industrial Revolution, modern medicine and the computer age. Yet it was hundreds of years after we applied it to steam, leeches and the stars that we finally started to use the same method to understand ourselves.

Why is there such a long fascination with the human mind, but such a very short scientific history of its study? We've always been fascinated by the weather, but climate science has been around for much longer. Why does meteorology predate psychology?

I think the answer has been lurking behind every chapter in this book. Psychology, unlike the sciences of physics, chemistry and biology, has a nemesis. It has an enemy that thwarts its progress at every turn: it has to deal with common sense.

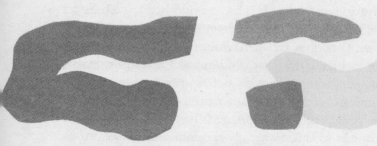

If I tell people about my research at a dinner party, I often hear something along the lines of, '*I could have told you that!*' in response. As the comedian David Mitchell, discussing the psychological finding that people gain weight when they are sad, once noted: 'It's really just common sense expensively turned into science.' '*I could have told you that*' is rarely heard by physicists when explaining wave-particle duality over the soup course.

This self-assured swagger of common sense is one of the reasons it took psychology so long to even begin as a science. Why would we need to do experiments to know ourselves? We spend our days with other people and dwell in our own thoughts, so we felt like we had the answers already.

However, psychological science has repeatedly confounded what seems like common sense. As we have seen, people do not value things for which they are rewarded. Through the tortuous logic of cognitive dissonance, they love that for which they suffer. Although we feel confident that we know the world around us at this moment in time, vision science shows that we are actually aware of the narrowest spotlight of attention. Our memories are not recordings of the past, but stories that are rehashed and fabricated with each retelling. No matter how sincerely we express our belief in fairness and equality, our behaviour can reveal the ugliest of stereotypes.

These days, we even have a good scientific understanding of common sense itself. Give people a set of statements that psychological science has proved to be true ('opposites attract' or 'picking up a crying baby too much makes it cry more', for example) and ask people to rate how much they agree with their common

The human mind is
not something that
seeks accuracy;
it seeks meaning

sense. Most will rate them as endorsing what they knew anyway. Then give another set of people the logically opposite statements ('people like others who are similar to themselves' or 'always pick up a crying baby'); in exactly the same way, they will confidently endorse them as being in agreement with their common sense. That's the trouble with common-sense beliefs: like toddlers and politicians, they feel no obligation to be consistent.

Confirmation bias is the engine behind common sense. After people are presented with a fact as truth, they search their knowledge for things to confirm it. Perhaps when David Mitchell read a psychology study about people gaining weight when they're sad, he thought of the sitcom trope of a character reaching for a tub of ice cream if they get dumped. This image confirms that finding as common sense. Equally, if the finding had been that people *lose* weight when they're sad, Mitchell could have visualised someone pining for a loved one while pushing away a plate of food. In hindsight, both these findings can seem equally valid, but that is the exact opposite of the scientific method, where two contradictory things cannot be true. Presented with something as fact, scientists seek out data to disconfirm the theory.

At the root of common-sense judgments is wisdom in hindsight, which is what we have seen repeatedly in this book. The human mind is not something that seeks truth and accuracy; it seeks meaning. We invent reasons for our own actions so that they make sense, so that dissonance is soothed away. We reconstruct our memories from fragments so they tell a coherent story. We explain the behaviour of other people in terms of their character, their disposition or their DNA, as that is a simpler plot than the knot of complex situational forces that actually governs behaviour. Man versus mind is a struggle precisely because we have to use careful experiments to untangle the simplifying stories we tell ourselves. This is why common sense is the nemesis of psychological science, and also why I hate dinner parties.

Acknowledgements

I would like to thank Natasha, for being an inspiring scientist and partner, and Sam, Calla and Isaac, the three minds that we have been studying and experimenting upon since their birth.

Sources

p.16 'You, your joys… Crick F. *The Astonishing Hypothesis: the Scientific Search for the Soul*, Simon & Schuster, London, 1994

p.27 One woman reported… Penfield W. 'Memory Mechanisms', *Archives of Neurology & Psychiatry*, 67 (2), 1952, pp. 178-198.

p.51 An experiment was done… Simons DJ & Levin DT. 'Failure to detect changes to people during a real-world interaction', Psychonomic Bulletin & Review, Vol. 5, 1988, pp. 644-649

you can find the video on YouTube… youtu.be/FWSxSQsspiQ

p.57 Eye-tracking work… Ballard DH, Hayhoe MM & Pelz JB. 'Memory Representations in Natural Tasks', *Journal of Cognitive Neuroscience*, Vol. 7, Iss. 1, 1995, pp. 66-80.

p.62 The fact-checking website… www. politico.com/magazine/story/2017/01/ donald-trump-lies-liar-effect-brain-214658

p.64 Researchers showed these… Kahan DM, Peters E, Dawson EC & Slovic P. 'Motivated Numeracy and Enlightened Self-Government', *Behavioural Public Policy*, Vol. 1, 2013, pp. 54-86.

p.67 A psychology professor… Friedrich J. 'On Seeing Oneself as Less Self-Serving than Others: The Ultimate Self-Serving Bias?', *Teaching of Psychology*, Vol. 23, Iss. 2, 1996, pp. 107-109.

p.68 Steve returned to his… Eibach RP and Mock SE. 'Idealizing Parenthood to Rationalize Parental Investments', *Psychological Science*, Association for Psychological Science, Vol. 22, Iss. 2, 2011, pp. 203-208.

p.72 The psychologist and his… Festinger L, Riecken HW & Schachter S. *When Prophecy Fails*, University of Minnesota Press, Minneapolis, 1956.

p.74 In a classic study,… Festinger L & Carlsmith JM. 'Cognitive Consequences of Forced Compliance', *The Journal of Abnormal and Social Psychology*, Vol. 58 (2), 1959, pp. 203-210.

p.75 As Festinger put it,… youtu.be/ DF4gdOlP-fc

p.78 In one of my favourite experiments… Johansson P, Hall L, Tärning B, Sikström S & Chater N. 'Choice Blindness and Preference Change: You Will Like This Paper Better If You (Believe You) Chose to Read it!', *Journal of Behavioral Decision Making*, Vol. 27, Iss. 3, 2014, pp. 281-289.

p.80 In a real supermarket,… Hall L, Johansson P, Tärning B, Sikström S & Deutgen T. 'Magic at the marketplace: Choice blindness for the taste of jam and the smell of tea', *Cognition*, Vol. 117, Iss. 1, 2010, pp. 54-61.

During a local election… Hall L, Strandberg T, Pärnamets P, Lind A, Tärning B & Johansson P. 'How the Polls Can Be Both Spot On and Dead Wrong: Using Choice Blindness to Shift Political Attitudes and Voter Intentions', *PLoS ONE*, Volume 8, 2013

p.86 This appears to be Gladstone's… Gladstone WE. *Studies on Homer and the*

Homeric Age, Oxford University Press, London, 1858.

p.91 We typically think of him... Keynes JM. 'Newton, The Man', *The Collected Writings of John Maynard Keynes, Volume 10: Essays in Biography*, Ch. 35, Royal Economic Society, London, 1978.

p.109 Munroe also looked... blog.xkcd.com/2010/05/03/color-survey-results/

p.111 It is known as... Whorf BL. *Language, Thought and Reality*, ed. Carroll, MIT Press, Cambridge, Massachusetts, 1956

p.115 The facts presented are... Pullum GK. *The Great Eskimo Vocabulary Hoax and Other Irreverent Essays on the Study of Language*, The University of Chicago Press, Chicago, 1991.

p.116 As Martin said about... Martin, L. '"Eskimo Words For Snow": A Case Study in the Genesis and Decay of an Anthropological Example', *American Anthropologist*, Vol. 88, No. 2, 1986, pp. 418-423.

p.118 Cognitive scientist Lera... Boroditsky L. 'How Language Shapes Thought', *Scientific American*, February 2011.

p.121 Boroditsky carried out experiments... Winawer J, Witthoft N, Frank MC, Wu L, Wade AR & Boroditsky, L. 'Russian blues reveal effects of language on color discrimination', *PNAS*, Vol. 104, No. 19, 2007, pp. 7780-7785.

p.131 They gave people a scale... Henry PJ & Sears DO. 'The Symbolic Racism 2000 Scale', *Political Psychology*, Vol. 23, No. 2, International Society of Political Psychology, 2002, pp. 253-283.

In a field study in the 1930s... LaPiere RT. 'Attitudes vs. Actions', *Social Forces*, Vol. 13, No. 2, 1934, pp. 230-237.

p.133 In one case, researchers... Norenzayan A & Schwarz N. 'Telling what they want to know: participants

tailor causal attributions to researchers' interests', *European Journal of Social Psychology*, Vol. 29, 1999, pp. 1011-1020.

If they were asked... Loftus EF. 'Leading Questions and the Eyewitness Report', *Cognitive Psychology*, Vol. 7, 1975, pp. 560-572.

p.134 Only twenty-two per cent... Henry PJ, Reyna C & Weiner B. 'Hate Welfare But Help the Poor: How the Attributional Content of Stereotypes

p.136 She was an orphan... www.vanityfair.com/news/2004/11/mccain200411

p.141 In one experiment,... Wojnowicz MT, Ferguson MJ, Dale R & Spivey MJ. 'The Self-Organization of Explicit Attitudes', *Psychological Science*, The Association for Psychological Science, Vol. 20, No. 11, 2009, pp. 1428-1435.

p.143 In one study,... FitzGerald C & Hurst S. 'Implicit bias in healthcare professionals: a systematic review', *BMC Medical Ethics*, Vol. 18, 2017.

p.152 In one experiment,... Chapman LJ & Chapman JP. 'Illusory correlation as an obstacle to the use of valid psychodiagnostic signs', *Journal of Abnormal Psychology*, Vol 74, 1969, pp. 271-280.

p.158 They then sent... www.theguardian.com/us-news/2015/dec/11/senator-ted-cruz-president-campaign-facebook-user-data

p.170 Two psychologists,... Jones EE & Harris VA. 'The Attribution of Attitudes', *Journal of Experimental Social Psychology*, Vol. 3, 1967, pp. 1-24.

p.171 In another experiment,... Ross LD, Amabile TM & Steinmetz J. 'Social Roles, Social Control and Biases in Social Perception Processes', *Journal of Personality and Social Psychology*, Vol. 35, 1977, pp. 485-494.

p.176 ...power of the situation. Milgram S. *Obedience to Authority: an experimental view*, Tavistock Publications, London, 1974.

p.181 One summer, psychology... Haney C, Banks WC & Zimbardo PG. 'A study of prisoners and guards in a simulated prison', *Naval Research Review*, Vol. 30, 1973, pp. 4-17.

p.188 As the writer Malcolm Gladwell... Gladwell M. *Outliers: The Story of Success*, Allen Lane, London, 2008.

p.189 He stated in a deposition... www. washingtonpost.com/politics/2016/ live-updates/general-election/real-time-fact-checking-and-analysis-of-the-first-presidential-debate/fact-check-how-much-help-did-trumps-father-give-his-son

p.193 Though the majority... www. theguardian.com/world/2015/apr/12/ uk-one-of-worlds-least-religious-countries-survey-finds

One in ten claims... yougov.co.uk/ news/2014/10/31/ghosts-exist-say-1-3-brits/

p.206 'When I first heard... Winograd E & Neisser U. *Affect and Accuracy in Recall: Studies of 'Flashbulb' Memories* (Emory Symposia in Cognition), Cambridge University Press, Cambridge, 1992.

p.208 George W Bush, the... Greenberg DL. 'President Bush's false [flashbulb] memory of 9/11/01', *Applied Cognitive Psychology*, Vol. 18, Iss. 3, 2004, pp. 363-370.

Donald Trump, the... www. washingtonpost.com/news/wonk/ wp/2015/11/24/donald-trump-might-not-be-lying-about-people-cheering-on-911

p.214 As the comedian David Mitchell... www.theguardian.com/ commentisfree/2009/jan/04/david-mitchell-is-worried